Brain-friendly Teacher

Yanina Jimenez

Copyright © 2022 Yanina Jimenez

All rights reserved.

ISBN: 978-0-578-28826-0

Disclaimer: This book is a compilation of research studies and findings from the Cognitive Psychology and Educational Neuroscience fields. The advice and strategies found within may not be suitable for every situation in your classroom. This work is sold with the understanding that neither the author nor the publisher are held responsible for the results accrued from the advice in this book.

Hello Teaching & Learning LLC

DEDICATION

To Diego, Gloria, and Andrés.
You are everything to me.

And to **you**, amazing teacher, for wanting your students to have a meaningful and lasting learning experience.

Contents

Hello, Amazing Teacher!   vii

1. **Another Person's Brain Changed My Life Forever**   1
2. **Chapter 2: Friends or Strangers?**   5
   Engage your students' brains
   Focusing your students' brains
   Calming your students' brains
3. **Brain-friendly Classroom (and Home) Design**   13
   That engages your students' brains
   That focuses your students' brains
   That calms your students' brains
4. **Brain-friendly Instructional Strategies**   41
   That engage your students' brains
   That focus your students' brains
   That calm your students' brains
5. **Practical Instructional Strategies to Create Lasting Learning**   61
   That engage your students' brains
   That focus your students' brains
   That calm your students' brains

6	How do my Students Learn, Really?	143
7	Brain-friendly Classroom Atmosphere	159
8	My Teacher Smiles	199
9	About the Author	203
10	Acknowledgments	207
11	References	211

Endorsements

"A must-read for everyone who works in education! Yanina has the ability to explain things in a very practical and creative way while giving you specific and effective learning strategies to enhance meaningful learning in your classroom. I know you'll find this book fascinating!"

Cynthia Hurtado-Muller. M.A. in Educational Neuropsychology, M.Sc. in Psychopathology and Health Psychology. Instagram: @neurofyok, Chile

"Yanina's ideology is heaven-sent for all educators around the world! She is the epitome of what being a 21st-century teacher looks like. Her passion and love for teaching just outpours so much that we all get to benefit from it! Please continue being an inspiration to all the teachers out there, and congratulations on this legendary creation of yours!"

Mary Jane Co, Preschool Educator from the Philippines

"Yanina Jimenez is a gift to our profession. She provides the science and strategies that are practical and easy to implement to make student learning meaningful and long-lasting. I am thrilled she is sharing her knowledge with all of us in her book Brain-Friendly Teacher and I pray you are as inspired by her work as I have been!"

Julie Adams @Adamsteaching Best Selling Author. NBCT, International Keynote Speaker, CA Educator of the Year

"Whenever Yanina shares or presents, teachers find her presentations so helpful. She's engaging, incredibly knowledgeable, but warm and approachable on a topic that can often be hard to break down into simple, actionable steps. Teachers can take advice from Yanina and instantly transform their learning space to work with their efforts and make everything about teaching easier, including the aspects of teaching that aren't often taught or talked about - learning space design and working with the ways the brain naturally learns. Yanina makes research easy to grasp in step-by-step instructions that any teacher can easily use."

Devon Gunning, La Libre Language Learning, World Language Conferences + Curriculum

"Becoming a brain-friendly teacher can seem overwhelming and complex. In this book, Yanina does what she does best - translate the complexities of how the brain learns into simple, practical, and tangible strategies you can implement in your classroom today."

Liesl McConchie, co-author of the best-selling book Brain-Based Learning. www.LieslMcConchie.com

"When looking for brain-friendly strategies based on the true science of teaching and learning, Yanina Jimenez is pioneering the way for the field of education with her new book, Brain-Friendly Teacher. If you are in the field of education, you'll know that it's been a transition to implement brain strategies in the classroom and you might wonder where to begin to teach with the brain in mind. Yanina's work takes the mystery out of science-based learning, with applicable strategies you can use right away (from brain-friendly classroom design, instructional strategies, and tips for creating a classroom atmosphere that engages, energizes, focuses, and calms your students' brains). If you are looking for cutting-edge ideas that will move the needle with student learning and infuse your classroom with a new energy, I highly recommend this book, and following Yanina's work."

Andrea Samadi
Host of the Neuroscience Meets Social and Emotional Learning podcast at Achieveit360.com

"Yanina jump-started my deep dive into understanding how brain anatomy and physiology have an important relationship in student learning. I love the conferences and resources she has curated, which have helped me design professional development for my coworkers."

Heidi Krusenklaus
Career Coordinator Elkhart Area Career Center

"Yanina is not only a passionate teacher and a brain lover, she's an inspirational source of meaningful information. Sometimes I feel that there's no more to learn about the brain, pedagogy, and psychology; and then I found Yanina's books, conferences, reels, and everything she shares. And, as I said before, she inspires teachers to become neuro-teachers! To learn about the science of learning, to be aware of the importance of a white wall in the classroom (just to mention one of the thousand tips that blew my mind), to let students be the owners of their learning process and know what is going on inside their brains when they are learning. So, this ultimate guide to becoming a brain-friendly teacher will help you boost up all the inner power that relies on every teacher, and Yanina has designed the perfect tool to help you!"

Magali Moser, EFL teacher. Buenos Aires - Argentina

"I've been following you for a while and I've loved the content you share. It is practical, evidence-based, and easy for educators to incorporate into their classrooms. Your book is a great addition to my library of resources for educators!"

Dr. Suzette Mirabal from Puerto Rico, Author of "Construye y diviértete con Neironi" www.brainconnections.co

"I have truly fallen in love with the message that she preaches. It has impacted my teaching life, my personal life, and my parenting on so many different levels and helped me to fully appreciate and identify with being neurodivergent. Thank you for this information and for everything that you do, Yanina! Please, continue to learn and grow and share what you are working on, as I have become an avid follower! Carry on, fellow educator! You are doing great things!!!"

Sarah Mason Isgrig, The Lesson Plans for Living

"As teachers, we frequently get caught up in the "do, do, do" mentality, for many reasons, especially when students struggle. It's a trap that's easy to fall into. Having Yanina as a resource to help me understand the brain science behind the learning has been invaluable in helping me to look beyond what a child is struggling with to gain insight into the WHY and to guide me to understand HOW to be a better educator."

Lisa Kincer @KincerLisa and @MrsKincersClass on Twitter and IG 3rd grade. Ireland Elementary Greater Jasper Consolidated Schools. Indiana

"Yanina's contributions to education, focusing on brain-friendly activities and Neuroscience of learning are remarkable and a game-changer. Her step-by-step approach and timely interventions are changing the narrative of teaching and learning across the world. Her passion and mastery in the realms of literalism make her stand out among her peers and reading her literary works are pleasantly addictive."

Michael Takyi, Teacher Trainer at OneSeed in Ghana, Africa.
Instagram: takyim and Facebook: Takyi Michael

"I run a private language school, and your ideas help me help the other teachers I work with. They are usually short and sweet, very helpful tips! Love them!"

Gabriela Ferrero, Educator from Argentina.

"As an educator, I have had the privilege of learning from Yanina through her online courses and our personal discussions. From purposeful classroom setup to instruction guided by cognitive neuroscience, Yanina continues to provide the best practical and relevant tips and advice for a successful brain-friendly classroom. My pedagogy has strengthened because of Yanina's research-based teachings. In her book, Yanina shows educators how to inspire a thirst for knowledge within their students by transforming their classrooms into optimal learning environments."

Sarah Sarah Rahimi, M.Ed.
4th grade International Baccalaureate Teacher

"I've been inspired by Yanina's classroom design and the tools she uses to inspire and engage her students."

Lisa Rhodes, Teacher

"Yanina is such an inspiration to many teachers and me. I love her work! I have used her ideas in the classroom and it has worked wonders. All of Yanina's work is very intentional and for the best of the students. Love her!"

Giovanna Wells, Educator.

"Yanina is a treasure in the field of brain-based learning. She places value on her students and takes great care in creating learning environments that support brain-friendly techniques!"

Tina Gabel, www.TeachTheTKWay.com

"Yanina's work on education is truly inspiring. She gets to other teachers' hearts by sharing her knowledge and making it so simple for us to put her ideas into practice."

Maria Francisca Kelly, founder of Bukku Education. Chile.

"Yanina is an inspirational educator from being in the classroom with her students and sharing her knowledge with other educators. She brings in so much love and connection while understanding how to set up her classroom for her students to grow and learn. I highly recommend adding her ideas to your classroom to make the best environment for everyone."

Michele Aloisio, Strength-Based Behavioral Consultant. www.sunshinethroughmotion.com

"Yanina is an amazing educator! I have had the pleasure of learning useful brain tips, which I apply regularly as a homeschool parent. When my child was in school, she thrived in Yanina's class. I am confident that anyone who reads this book will glean gems of information that can be applied both in and out of the classroom."

Ru McKenzie, MBA www.justbeconfident.com

"Yanina has shared such helpful, easy tips for teaching every type of learner over the last couple of years. Her knowledge and sincere love of her craft are known with every suggestion. I am so excited for you all to read through this book and apply it with ease!"

Dana Skillman, 4th-grade teacher @smilingwithscience
Owner and creator of @chasinselfcare

"Your work has been really supportive and inspiring for my teaching practice! Thank you so much for your kind emails full of wonderful tips!"

Vanessa, Educator. Instagram: @vanessadiaz2572

"Yanina is all heart. Her work is practical and functional, but layered with ease and wildly digestible for educators. She doesn't simply provide actionable tips to increase learning and retention based on brain science. She weaves the WHY into everything she teaches in an effort to empower educators to begin thinking more deeply about HOW students learn. I am so proud of her for this incredible work and honored to continue being a student of hers."

Rachel Nye, Founder of Safe Space Teaching

"I met Yanina through Instagram and through a friend who knows I am always looking for a new way to teach my students about how the brain works. I started following her, then we started talking more and more. Every post that she does has been an inspiration for me to try it in my classroom. I have learned so much from her and the workshop I attended once. I have also purchased her course and learned a lot more. She has inspired me to purchase more books about the study of the brain to understand how the learning child thinks and to help my students in a better way. Thank you, Yanina, for your amazing job! I am so excited to be able to read your book."

Sarai Sanchez, Educator.

"Yanina has an inspiring way to make neuroscience applicable in the classroom through many simple yet effective activities and tips that she shares on her IG account. That's why I follow her and I think her content is so valuable to the teaching community."

Gina Rodriguez, Educational consultant, and digital marketing specialist www.grschoolmarketing.com

"Yanina's work guides all teachers, no matter their subject area, into the fields of neuroscience in a simple and practical way. Her constant research provides us, teachers, with hands-on activities to promote better learning in all our classes. This book is a must-have for teachers concerned with Brain-Friendly teaching."

Eugenia DellOsa, from @plan.up.education in Argentina. plan.up.educational.advisor@gmail.com

"I have followed and engaged with Yanina for many years now. Her amazing tips and resources have taught me so much about the science of learning in a really easy-to-understand way that I can bring straight into my practice! It has helped me better understand myself and those around me which has improved relationships personally and professionally! Thanks, Yanina."

- **Naomi Toland**, PLD Facilitator, and Teacher. New Zealand
NaomiToland.com, Twitter @naomi_toland

Brain-friendly Teacher

Hello, amazing teacher!

I know you are an amazing teacher because you are holding yet another book on teaching strategies! Aha! I don't need any more proof than that! I know you spend time thinking about the best ways to teach a lesson. And after you have taught that lesson, you wonder if that lesson stuck in your students' brains! I know you spend a lot of time searching all over the web and social media for the best activities that match that lesson, standard, or unit. You finally find an activity you like, you think your students will love it too, and you even pay for it! You try it and then wonder again if your students really remember what you taught them!

That is why I am sure you are going to love this book and find it very useful. So useful that you will always have it on your teacher's desk or by your laptop at the time of planning your lessons, and at the time of designing your classroom – because that too impacts the student's learning experience.

This book is based on research, therefore is full of principles that you can apply to all your lessons. Principles that come directly from the science of teaching and learning. Principles for knowledge and skills to stick in your students' long-term memory! Use this book as a constant reference. Apply these principles to everything you teach and do in your classroom!

No more wondering about what works and what doesn't! You will be able to choose strategies based on the science of learning. Strategies that will help your students remember what you teach and become life-long learners!

If you are like me, you didn't take courses in college about the science of learning or how the **learning brain** works. You fell in love with this after you started teaching. For me, my curiosity and love for brain science started with an abrupt experience when I was 10…

Chapter 1: How Another Person's Brain Changed my Life Forever

After some terrible news I received one day, I lost everything in a matter of months, or so it seemed to me as a 10-year-old girl…

I lost my parents,

my sister,

my house,

my friends,

my school,

my house,

my bedroom,

my culture,

my sense of belonging,

my way of going to school - from riding a bus to riding a horse!

my church,

my routines,

my health,

my family,

my furniture,

my neighbors,

my lifestyle…

Everything…

My family and I knew my dad couldn't keep driving in his condition. His neurologist told him and my mom that. His job required a lot of driving, so we knew that a change was coming. But, the change came suddenly during a visit to his doctor. The neurologist told him he couldn't leave the office with his driving license. His brain issue could provoke an accident at any time, and it could end in a tragedy for him or anyone on the road.

My dad came home and told us that he couldn't work anymore. We were living in Uruguay at that time. Both my mom and my dad were from Argentina, so we packed up and traveled back to their home country to visit my grandfather. I remember their conversations under the beautiful fruit trees on that dreamy farm. It was my happy place. I loved visiting it, riding horses and his tractor, and playing barefooted around the dogs, cows, horses, and chickens.

The conversation at that time, though, was different. Even though I was playing with my brother and sister, I could still see their worried faces.

How Another Person's Brain Changed My Life Forever

After a few hours of serious conversations, they came up with a plan. "We are returning to Uruguay, only to get everything ready to move here, Argentina!" Mom and dad told us that day. We went back to Uruguay after those few days in Argentina and indeed all the plans started. We started selling everything. My brother and I were in school, so they decided to let us finish our school year in Uruguay. They moved to Argentina while we still had a few more weeks of school to finish in Uruguay. They went with my little sister to Argentina so they could start building our future house and start a new business.

And just like that, they put our house up for sale. They moved first to Argentina, and we stayed behind with a nanny for a few weeks until our school ended. During this time, I felt like I had lost absolutely everything and that my world had completely changed forever. My little sister went with them, but my brother stayed with me. We missed our parents and our little sister so much.

Since then, I couldn't help but be astonished by how much an issue in someone else's brain can change the whole course of a family's life. I soon became obsessed with the brain. At that time, I didn't have a research bar on the internet to look for brain facts and information to understand what was going on.

Years later, I went to a university to study music and education. I remember going to the library to work on my assignments. After I'd finished them, I would go to the brain anatomy textbooks and find myself in awe of this amazing organ. In those moments, I sometimes felt like I was betraying my majors because I was still in love with neuroscience. For this reason, I kept these two areas very separated from each other, never imagining that they could be friends! After all, I never took a neuroscience class in college. I know many teachers like me have experienced the same fascination with the brain, but don't always have college classes that help them understand the relationship between brain science and the process of teaching and learning.

Ironic, right? Learning happens in the brain!

After I graduated, my husband and I came to the United States, where I completed my Master's in Curriculum and Instruction. One afternoon, my professor told me, "I notice you really enjoy writing about the brain!" I now know that this passion has a name: educational neuroscience, psychology of learning, cognitive neuroscience, or science of teaching and learning. "In your next research class, you can start writing about something you really like!"

That day, everything changed for me again. I came full circle! I realized that education and neuroscience could go together. That might seem super obvious to some, but it never was for me until that moment. That day, I felt like I finally had permission to talk, read, write, research, and go after what I had always wanted. My passion was not only permitted; it was now possible!

That day, I felt like I could be in love with two different fields, and that was OK! I realized that even if those two fields were not best friends yet, I would do my best to tell teachers the good news, which is that the psychology of learning has so much to offer to us as teachers and our students. The science of teaching and learning is all about applying simple strategies, based on brain science, in order for students to experience meaningful and lasting learning! We now know how to bring knowledge, concepts, and skills to our students' long-term memory. There is no more guessing about what works and what doesn't. We don't have to follow all the trends. Brain-friendly classroom design and instruction are not rocket science. When you apply these simple principles, lasting learning does happen! And I know you want your students to experience this!

In the next chapter, the only "nerdy" one, you will go behind scenes to see the relationship between researchers and teachers and how this directly impacts **you and your students**. Yes, I know, that crucial!

Chapter 2: Friends or Strangers?

Less recess,

No art time,

More time on screen,

Long hours sitting still,

Left-brained,

Right-brained,

Learning styles,

And so many other infiltrated brain myths into teaching practices, are some of the consequences of two entities that seem strangers to each other. Even though the education system, at times, seems to be a stranger to brain science and brain science, at times, a stranger to the education system, you can still be a brain-friendly teacher! You can still have brain-friendly practices when it comes to classroom design, instruction, and classroom atmosphere. As you read about this distant relationship, I don't want you to lose hope. I want you to be aware of what is going on between the laboratory, where scholars research, and the classroom, where teachers teach. That way you can see where you stand and how you can do even better for your students!

Before we get to all the practical tips for a brain-friendly classroom design, instruction, and atmosphere in the following chapters, let's take a closer look at what is happening between the lab and the classroom.

Ready? Let's go straight to it!

"Neuroscientists lament that they know certain things about how to improve learning but the field of education is not responding," while teachers say that they are the ones who know best what works in their classrooms (Zadina, 2015). This situation is described by Bruer (1997) as a "bridge too far" from each other. Teachers say that neuroscientists do not speak the language of educators who are in classrooms, and neuroscientists argue that teachers are not listening to research results on which to base their practices.

The ideal solution?

Ideally, scientists and teachers need to be friends and have a two-way conversation. They need to talk and listen to each other!

Ideally, neuroscientists need to come to classrooms and see firsthand if what they say works or not. They can test their findings and gain useful feedback from classroom teachers and students. They can also see how teachers deal with diverse and struggling students. Even if it looks pretty or perfect in theory, scientists need to hear and act on classroom teachers' feedback.

Ideally, teachers need to be experts on how the brain learns. Teachers need to have more access to books and training based on the science of teaching and learning so students can have a meaningful and lasting learning experience. After all, we are trusted to teach students in the best way possible, which is by understanding the process and science of teaching and learning. But, this is not our fault as teachers, not at all!

Remember when I shared before that when I was in college I felt like cheating on my Education Major, by reading brain anatomy textbooks? I did that because I never had a class in college that taught me how learning happens in the brain. I never had a class that explained the effect of classroom design on students' minds. I never had a class that would classify instructional strategies by brain needs. I remember that most of the classes were based on psychology and pedagogy, which were great. I wish, though, I would have had classes based on neuroscience too. Neuroscience has much to offer us as teachers. For example, there are brain images and studies that shed so much light on how neurons work together so students can have a lasting learning experience. Isn't that so cool? I find it fascinating!

Since teachers don't know or don't get to read and be familiarized with the latest research findings in the science of teaching and learning, we "tend to rely on our intuitions about how to teach and learn with detrimental consequences" (Weinstein, Sumeracki, Caviglioli, 2019, pg. 3). They also say that since our own intuitions are not always correct, they can lead us to pick the wrong learning strategies. When we are not familiarized with the science of teaching and learning, we end up listening to many entities who are competing to be the authorities in the field of education such as politicians, textbook companies, administrators, media… you name it.

We, teachers, need to listen to experts who have a foot in the classroom and another foot in research. "We need a specialist with a foot on each side" (Howard-Jones, 2010). The ones on this bridge need to love both sides and not argue with one side. These people are called educational neuroscientists (also called cognitive psychologists or researchers in the science of teaching and learning). These academic neuroscientists understand the language of scientists and educators. They love theory, and they love to practice their findings. These experts in the science of teaching and learning can inform both sides, researchers and teachers, in their respective languages.

The reality?

Sadly, we know that this is not happening quite yet, because we are seeing the effects of this disconnection in education. This can be either because neuroscience is not talking to classroom teachers, or classroom teachers are not listening to brain science. But why do teachers are not listening to brain science? This is why: "The science of learning sits dormant in academic journals, rather than easily accessible in per-service textbooks and professional development materials" (Agarwal & Bain, 2019).

You and I have proof that there is a lack of communication because schools are cutting art and music instruction even when brain science shows how crucial these skills are for students. Another important element that budget cuts have taken out of our students' learning experience is recess and free play. Movement is vital to memory, for engaging/energizing, focusing, and calming students' brains.

Administrations not advised by neuroscience are also handing down third-handed brain research. Neuromyths are still being perpetuated, such as the right and left brain. I am sure that you have seen brain images where one side is black and white and the other side is super colorful. I understand if those images are from decades ago, but if those images are recent, I tend to discard that book or article altogether! That picture itself is a myth! Our brain, on the contrary, is "incredibly dynamic, with multiple interconnected networks engaged" (Posey, 2019, pg. 71). Another consequence of not following neuroscience's findings is having classrooms over-decorated. This clutter or walls affects how our students think, learn, and behave. These myths and so many others are brought to the classroom through counterproductive instructional strategies, classroom design, and management. In the following chapters, you will have tons of practical brain-friendly tips for each one of those areas! Good things ahead!

What can you do?

Well, you are doing something about it already by reading this book and the other amazing books cited in the following chapters. In this book, you will find hundreds of practical strategies based on the science of teaching and learning. No more guessing or looking just for an activity that matches your lesson. You will find simple strategies to help your students encode, consolidate, and retrieve information from their brains. Your teaching and your students' learning experience will be transformed!

Keep this book as a constant reference in your classroom, on your teacher's desk, or by your laptop at the time of choosing instructional strategies to teach a lesson or a unit or designing your classroom - which needs to happen more than once a year! Oh, and have some cute highlighters at hand too!

In this book, you will get practical and powerful proven principles for:
1. a brain-friendly classroom design
2. a brain-friendly instruction and
3. a brain-friendly classroom atmosphere.

Classroom design, instruction, and classroom atmosphere need to
- engage/energize
- focus and
- calm your students' brains.

In each chapter, you will read about the importance of engaging/energizing, focusing, and calming your students' brains. Brains need this cycle for authentic, meaningful, and lasting learning.

Why engage and energize your students' brains?

Students come to our school, classroom, and classes many times tired, still sleepy, and in their own world. We know this! As soon as our students enter our classrooms, we need to engage their brains. When we energize and engage their brains, they are more alert and ready to receive what we need to teach them! In this book, you will get a toolbox of ideas to engage your students' brains through classroom design and instruction.

Why focus your students' brains?

Students need to focus in order to tackle new and complex concepts or skills. They need to be able to sustain focused attention. This can't happen by simply telling them, "Pay attention!" as soon as they enter our classrooms. We need to engage them first, and then, after we have their attention, we can help them focus. In this book, you will have at hand hundreds of proven techniques to focus your students' minds through classroom design and instruction.

Why calm your students' brains?

We can't expect students to be full of energy and attention during the whole day or even during a whole class period. We need to provide the time and space for their brains to calm down. Calming our students' brains is not just about giving them time to rest. Calming our students' brains plays a crucial part in the consolidation of learning. Learning is like lifting weights; we need to warm up to hold the weights, and then bring the weights down and rest if we want to do another round of heavy lifting!

Friends or Strangers?

In this book, you will have all kinds of strategies to engage/energize, focus, and calm your students through classroom design and instruction.

Ready? Let's do this!

Brain-friendly Teacher

Chapter 3: Brain-friendly Classroom Design

"The function of design is letting design function." - Micha Commeren, designer

For every story, there is a setting, and for every experience, there is a place that makes it unique. And for learning is the same. Learning happens in a learning space! So let's talk about that space before we talk about instructional strategies that facilitate the drive of information from short-term to long-term memory, which is what learning is all about!

Your students are not affected nor benefited just from your instruction, your attitude, your classroom atmosphere, and your management. It is affected by the learning space too, by the ways you decorate it and set it up. Your classroom setup and décor play a crucial role in the learning experience. At the time of setting up your classroom, you need to think beyond a theme and cute accessories. No judgment here, I think about those things too! I used to love the phrase that the classroom was my kingdom and my space, but I realize now this can't be further from the truth. The classroom is your student's learning space. Your classroom sends a message even if you are not in it. It lets your students know about your values, your style, how you view learning, diversity, and so many other important things!

Since your students are going to spend about 1,400 hours in your classroom during a school year, it is crucial to realize the impact of those four walls, furniture, organization, flow, colors, scents, etc. on your students' brains. Your classroom space affects how your students **"think, feel, and behave** in myriad ways" (Hetland, 2007, cited by Ostroff, 2016). Moreover, the classroom environment is sometimes referred to as another teacher.

Have you ever wondered what your students thought about **their** classroom when they entered it on the first day of school? How did that space make them feel?

Seen?
Understood?
Accepted?
Heard?
Excited?
Calm?
Focused?
Curious?
Challenged?
Energized?
Engaged?
Safe?
Loved?

Your learning space is **all** about your learners.

There is even more to it!!! A recent research study found that teachers who regularly modified and changed their classrooms to create better, more effective learning spaces were also more likely to use innovative pedagogies and collaborate with their colleagues (Bissell, 2004). Who knew that decorating our classrooms at the beginning of the school year was so crucial? Although we tend to think that designing our classrooms is about decoration, there is much more to think about besides a color palette, a theme, etc. We need to design it to serve our needs for true, meaningful, and lasting learning.

Brain-friendly Learning Spaces need to engage/energize, focus, and calm your students' brains.

Our classrooms have four walls, so my go-to formula to engage/energize, focus and calm my students' brains is 1+2+1!

ONE wall to engage your students' brains:

Set up a place, **one** wall, or a corner where you provide many things for your students to be creative while feeling engaged and energized. For example, put up bright posters, bright lights, etc. You don't have to put chairs in this space. If your students can do their projects while standing up, it will be much better for them! That way, you give the time and space to your students to **move**. Their brains will like that and will permit them to be more creative and enthusiastic about what they are doing: which is not just crafts but puppet shows, podcasts, commercials, STEM projects, etc.! This place can also have their **unfinished** projects displayed, instead of putting everything away because it is time to do something else!
More things to keep in mind to engage/energize your students:

Flow

> *"Design is not just what it looks like and feels like. Design is how it works."*
> *— Steve Jobs*

Your learning space needs to invite your learners to be engaged, and at the same time, they should feel energized to do their best, be productive and creative. The flow of your room is crucial to accomplishing these two brain needs. Create spaces for students to get easily from point A to B, from B to C, and so on. Avoid having things on the floor or hanging out that might be in the way of traffic in your classroom, between desks, furniture, bookshelves, and your stuff! When you look around in your room, ensure that you can easily see mini-hallways for your students to walk freely and with enough space to have two students walking in opposite directions! Reason it like this, "How would you like to enjoy "flow" in other spaces, such as your house, restaurants, shops, etc.?! If you like the flow of a space that you visit, get ideas and use them in your classroom. I get so many ideas from educational or STEM spaces located inside libraries and museums!

Movement

"All creative activity begins with movement." - Joseph C Zinker

Provide your students with opportunities to move. You do not need a flexible seating space to do this. So, if you only have desks in your classroom, you can put cushions on your student chairs and a band to move their feet! You can also put a box inside their desks filled with items that engage/energize, focus and calm your students' brains, such as brain toys, stress balls, pipe cleaners, etc. That way, they can have some fidgeting outlets! All my students have a STEAM box inside their desks and they love it!

If you have the opportunity to have a flexible seating space in your classroom, make sure you allow your students to enjoy different positions while working such as standing, kneeling, walking, bouncing, laying down, rocking, tummy touching the ground, back touching the ground, seating, seating, and feet up, etc. The key is to provide your students with opportunities to move and choose their optimum place and learning position. Make sure your learners move *while* learning and don't think of movement as a separate activity from learning. Students need to try many alternative positions throughout the day.

You can also let your students stand up while they work at a standing or tall desk. Just make sure your students change positions. It is not comfortable to stand up the whole day in one position, nor sit on a bouncy ball without back support for long periods of time. That is why allowing your students to change positions according to their needs is very important.

I love flexible seating, and we often associate this with sitting comfortably for hours. This is not bad, but the point of flexible seating is about options and movement, not an invitation to sit comfortably for hours without moving! There are many strategies for effective learning, such as music, emotions, hands-on, etc. But the number one thing the brain loves and needs is **movement.** Movement is "the most transformative thing you can do for your brain." This is the famous phrase from Wendy Suzuki in her TED Talk in 2018.

Suzuki also says in her TedTalk, that movement supplies brain cells with oxygen, promotes the production of new brain cells, and aids in creating new synapses. Movement increases energy, reduces stress, and calms the mind and body. Movement is also liked and needed by the hippocampus, and as a result, students can consolidate learning in their long-term memory. We truly want that!!!

Colors

"Color is a power which directly influences the soul." - Wassily Kandinsky

The psychology of color tells us that bright colors promote energy, and yellow is not the only color that can do this! You do not need to paint a whole wall with a bright color either. Just make sure you provide a space that invites and welcomes creativity, productivity, and energy. Dedicate a place, or a wall, in your classroom to engage and energize your students' brains. If the only thing you want to do with your space is to engage and energize your students' brains, then use the whole classroom to accomplish this. If you do, do it all with intense colors. Otherwise, just provide a space, a corner, and even a wall that invites your students to be creative and productive. This space can be your makerspace, which you will read about coming up. It can be a table with puzzles, hands-on things, manipulatives, or anything that fits with what you are teaching. That way, your students can be energized, engaged, productive, and creative.

Hailey van Braam (2021), on her amazing website (colorpsychology.org), talks about how each color affects humans. She says, "When it comes to communication, color is unbeatable. Unconscious or otherwise, color can evoke emotions, inspire reactions, and change modes of thinking."

Have you noticed that stores that sell healthier products use a lot of green and books that want to make a strong point, use red on their covers? Businesses know about the psychology and power of color. Look around and you will see that every color has a purpose! This is not a random decision! I used shades of pink for the cover of this book, because I want you to feel optimistic and understood when you open this book. Pink also means approachable and easy. That is exactly what I want to portray when I talk about Educational Neuroscience. I don't want to sound fancy and so sophisticated that you think this topic is boring or unrelatable, because it is not at all!

So, now think about the message of your classroom space and walls you want to send to your students! Remember not to use one color for the whole space. Divide your classroom into spaces to meet your students' needs. Your classroom needs to engage/energize, focus, and calm your students. Avoid the extremes, such as having all the walls displaying bright and laminated posters, or all the walls completely dull and empty! Use different colors to convey **your classroom message**. You don't need to use them all!

Use **red** to convey energy, strength, power, determination, and love.

Use **green** to convey freshness, growth, and calmness.

Use **blue** to convey enthusiasm and imagination.

Use **brown** to convey calmness, tranquility, and resiliency.

Use **orange** to convey energy, joy, and creativity.

Use **yellow** to convey joy, energy, and stimulation.

Use **pink** to convey tenderness, calmness, and optimism.

Use **purple** to convey wisdom and independence.

Use **white** to convey new beginnings, safety, and new beginnings.

Use **black** to convey power, elegance, formality, and strength.

Lights

"A room is not a room without natural light." – Louis Kahn

Is there a time in your day or during a class when you want students to be super active? Then, play with lights! Have them bright, or turn on all those string lights. Remember, though, that you can add filters to those lights so they don't affect you or your students. There is such a thing as being sensitive to loud noises and bright lights. A classroom setup can be overstimulating to our students. That is why you can never go wrong with natural light, so open those curtains and let the sun rays come into your classroom!

During the last century, school architects decided to design classrooms with small windows or no windows at all in an attempt to remove distractions so students could focus on their work. Imagine the anxiety of those children being in closed spaces! Now, architects are doing the opposite! They know natural light actually helps students focus! If you don't have natural light, try fluorescent light filters for your classroom.

Even if you do have big windows in your classroom, try to bring them outside as much as possible. They will enjoy the warmth of the sun and fresh air. Fresh and clean air are good for our brains. Your students will enjoy being outside and will be more awake too!

Collaborative space

"Alone we can do so little; together we can do so much." – Helen Keller

Collaborative time and space can happen when a group of students sits on group tables, flower tables, or a carpet on the floor where you have morning meetings and/or collaborations. If you have desks in rows and columns, make sure you also dedicate a space where your whole class or a group can meet. If your classroom is small, your students can take turns in this collaborative space.

In this collaborative space students can:
- meet as a group that has a few or many things in common
- sing a class song
- recite the class motto or mission

Displays

"The best rooms have something to say about the people who live in them."
– David Hicks

One day, an administrator came to my classroom to conduct a formal evaluation. Yes, I was nervous, yet everything went great in my mind! After the evaluation, she told me I had a lot of things on the walls. I admire and respect this person a lot. She is on the list of acknowledgments at the end of this book, actually! Even though I always admired her, this time what she said took me by surprise because I was convinced that all the posters and anchor charts I had on my walls, windows, bookshelves, and even the ceiling were necessary! Yes, the ceiling. I used cut-out green and bright letters to spell: "Capitalization and Punctuation!"

It took me months to make changes. I would take some things down and then put some other "necessary" things back. All this back and forth did change something in me. I started to realize that I indeed had too much on walls and literally everywhere. So, you know what I did? I took absolutely everything down, yes... everything. And I lived with it for a few days. I felt relaxed, and I actually liked it that way. Then, little by little, I started putting up only the things that my students needed to see during that particular unit or week and no extra décor. Now, I think 10 times before putting something on display!!! I recommend you do the same, take everything down and live with it a few days before starting putting things back.

It is better to display posters and other necessary things on one or two walls at the most and leave the other two for the other brains' needs, which are focusing and calming your students' minds. Display student work, goals, word wall, anchor charts, and whatever is extremely necessary and current to help your students energize their brains.

About student work:
- include everyone's work
- display drafts and polished pieces
- ask for input from students
- put pieces at eye level
- avoid lamination
- avoid clutter

Leave ample blank space around everything you display, and since displays can take up space rather quickly, I advise you to take everything down in your classroom. Live with it for a day or two or even longer. Finally, start putting things up after you decide they are extremely crucial to show to your students. You will see that now you have much less than before!

Makerspace

"Creativity is allowing yourself to make mistakes. Design is knowing which ones to keep." – Scott Adams

A makerspace is a wonderful and needed addition to your classroom! A makerspace is not just a place to do things. It is a place that represents curiosity, problem-solving, and trial and error. It is a place that invites students to create and try new things. In a classroom where there is a makerspace, students don't just consume content. They create meaningful things that extend learning. They can also manipulate ideas and concepts. They can see, touch, hear, and feel what they are learning. What they learn is no longer abstract and invisible, they can see their thinking and learning through the things they create!

Makerspaces/STEAM labs are not just places. Makerspaces are a mindset and a philosophy that advocate for the **creation of learning** and not just consumption. You can dedicate this space to extend learning and create just about anything for more subjects than just science and math. Students can make storyboards for stories, play with letters, build writing scenes and so much more. These are just some ideas you can try in your class. You don't even have to have expensive and fancy tech in a makerspace!

- 2-D Models
- 3-D Models
- Advertisements
- Animations
- Blogs
- Book illustrations
- Books written by themselves
- Books written as a class
- Books using paper bags
- Brochures
- Cartoons
- CD player with audiobooks
- Class books
- Collages
- Comedy Skits
- Commercials
- Concept Maps
- Data Analysis
- Debates
- Diary entries
- Digitally-Documented Discussion
- Diorama
- Doodling
- Drawing
- eBooks
- Escape Rooms or creation of escape rooms or challenges
- Experiments

- Exploration of Nature Objects
- Films
- Flashcards making for review
- Flipbooks
- Flow Charts
- Fun drilling basic operations
- Games
- Gif animations
- Glossaries
- Google Earth Tours
- Graphic Organizers
- Graphs
- Hexagonal Thinking
- Infomercials
- Instructional Conversations
- Interviews
- Jenga with words or activities on each stick
- Leave random letters to form words/sentences
- Letter formation
- Literature Circle
- Live Streams
- Logs
- Magazines
- Make simple machines
- Map Exploration
- Math concepts in action
- Mazes
- Mixtures and solutions
- Murals
- Musical instruments
- Newspapers
- Origamis
- Painting
- Panel Discussions

- Photography
- Physical science lessons in action
- Podcasts
- Poems
- Portfolios
- Punctuation and sentence structure using objects
- Puppet Shows
- Recordings
- Reenactments
- Robot making out of random parts or junk bot!
- Scavenger Hunts
- Scrapbooks
- Sculptures
- Short Videos
- Show & Tells
- Simulations
- Slide Shows
- Socratic Discussions
- Songs
- Sorting and classification
- Speeches
- Surveys
- Theatrical Plays
- Time Capsules
- Timelines
- Tutorials
- Velocity, speed, and other concepts using small cars
- Vloggs
- Websites
- Whiteboard Animations
- YouTube video creation or consumption

There is no limit when students are given the time and space to be creative! These are some of the objects that I have in my makerspace.

I try not to have kits, only loose parts so my students can create things from scratch. Make sure also the objects you put in this space are age-appropriate!

- Beads
- Binder clips
- Bottle caps
- Brushes
- Card stock
- Chalk
- Clay
- Construction paper
- Cups
- Glue
- Hot glue sticks
- Magnifying glasses
- Markers
- Microscope
- Paint
- Paper clips
- Pipe cleaners
- Popsicle sticks
- Rubber bands
- Scissors
- Stickers
- Straws
- Tape
- Yarn

And all the random things you can get at your house, a second-hand store, or any dollar place! More points if you can avoid plastic objects!

TWO walls to focus your students' brains:

To focus your students' brains, you need fewer displays on walls. Use one or two walls at the most to display things that will help your students focus on what they need to focus on. For example, if there is more than what is necessary on walls, students will not focus on what they need to focus on! Make sure you have white spaces. At least one wall should be empty.

Dedicated space to focus the brain

"It is nice finding that place where you can just go and relax." —Moises Arias

Once you know what your students must focus on, have a dedicated space for this. Your students will know exactly in which direction to look to be redirected to regain focus! When you place a few posters or anchor charts on these two walls, make sure that there is white space around those things. That way, when you need to redirect your students' attention to that chart, for example, they will not be distracted by the other charts that are super close to that one. Leave white/empty spaces between the few charts, posters, and anchor charts.

White spaces

"A life without a lonely place, that is, without a quiet center, becomes destructive." - Henri Nouwen

White spaces are necessary to help the brain understand and organize what it is absorbing. White spaces are not always white in design or instruction. White spaces are about making a space between information and activities, too. These are ten ways to use white spaces to meet your students' brain needs!

1. Leave white, blank, or solid spaces on walls. Whatever display is left needs to be as minimum as possible, so students can easily focus on what they need to focus on. The white space helps students better focus on what is not in the white space!
2. Leave a few minutes as white space between different subjects or classes, so students can reset to focus again!
3. Leave a few minutes within the class for students to understand, reflect, and organize what they are learning.
4. Leave white spaces on worksheets, don't fill it out to the maximum with cute clip art and extra decoration.
5. The white space has a fantastic ability to draw people to the elements you want them to focus on. So, whatever super important thing you want your students to focus on, leave white space around it before and after presenting it.
6. White spaces apply to space *and* to time.
7. White spaces eliminate distractions.
8. They separate and emphasize essential information.
9. White spaces only work in conjunction with display and instruction that help focus the brain.
10. Leave white spaces in your lectures, slides, lists, tests, assignments, in everything!

Dedicated space to calm the brain

"Wisdom grows in quiet places." - Austin O'Malley

Once you know what your students must focus on, have a dedicated space for this. Your students will know exactly in which direction to look to be redirected to gain focus again!

Students will be able to encode information in a clear and organized way in their long-term memory. We truly want that!!!

ONE wall to calm your students' brains:

Walls play a massive role in your learning space. Walls are thought of as the third teacher! Your walls should also contribute to bringing calmness to your students. You are going to use **one** wall to engage/energize your students' brains, **two** walls to display necessary things to focus your students' brains, and **one** to leave it completely blank, don't add anything extra to it. Or, you can use this fourth wall for displaying as minimum as possible. Please, try to have this wall as empty as possible. Your brain and your students' brains will thank you! Bring decoration and stuff to a minimum. Declutter, declutter, declutter! By this empty wall, you can provide a "calm corner."

Calm corners

"To be calm is the highest achievement of the self." - *Zen proverb*

Have you ever felt you had no other option but to push through a school day? Did you wish you had a place where you could just go for a minute and breathe deeply? Our students go through the same and they don't have the ability to switch to focusing mode as soon as they enter through our classroom door. As soon as they come, we expect them to be on, ready to learn, ready to engage in deep thinking, and ready to just think and work on their assignments. Imagine if they also have to deal with a problem at school with their friends. That is why it is so important to have a time-in, not time-out, corner. A safe place where they can just breathe, escape from the world, and regain mental and physical strength to push through the day. "A relaxation station is an essential component in every classroom to support sensory needs and self-regulation" (Maich, Davies, van Rhijn, 2018).

A calm down corner is a designated space in your classroom where students can go when they need to regulate their emotions. Calm down corners are becoming popular for their ability to help students implement social and emotional learning skills.

Find a good place for it so it can be a bit separate from the high traffic of your classroom. Add the following if you can!

- comfortable furniture
- a bean bag or a chair
- signs for breathing techniques
- things they can do in that space, such as strategies for dealing with problems, etc.
- calm down tools
- sensory toys
- Play-Doh
- kinetic sand
- a timer
- soft rug
- relaxation CDs
- CD player
- calm playlist
- headphones
- books
- magazines
- low partitions
- dividers for privacy
- visual calming strategies
- sensory bins
- neutral colors on the wall or corner
- objects from nature
- dim lights

Walls

"Every calm and quiet place is the true temple of the wise man!"
- Mehmet Murat Ildan

You need to use at least one wall to leave it completely blank, don't add anything extra to it. Again, try to leave it empty or use the minimum display possible. Your brain and your students' brains will thank you! If you can't afford to have a wall completely empty, you can use your windows for this purpose! Open those curtains too!

Wall colors

"Colors are the smiles of nature." Leigh Hunt

You don't have to paint one or two walls with a calm color. If you can, it would be nice, but this is not a must. However, you can still provide a corner where the colors used are more relaxed than the other corners in your classroom. Sometimes, we fall into the trap that the whole learning space should be calm. We can't do this and serve our students' brains efficiently. If you want to differentiate your calming space from your engaging space in your classroom, do it in different corners or areas! You can also change how they look and feel!

Uncluttered walls

"Simplicity is the ultimate sophistication." —Leonardo da Vinci

I wrote about this before, but "uncluttered walls" deserve a few extra paragraphs in this book! Maps, number lines, shapes, artwork, and other materials tend to cover elementary classroom walls. However, too much of a good thing may end up disrupting attention and learning in young children, according to a research published in the Journal of Psychological Science.

Psychology researchers Fisher, Godwin, and Seltman of Carnegie Mellon University looked at whether classroom displays affected children's ability to maintain attention during instruction and learn the lesson content. They found that children in highly decorated classrooms were more distracted, spent more time off-task, and demonstrated smaller learning gains than when the decorations were removed.

"Young children spend a lot of time — usually the whole day — in the same classroom, and we have shown that a classroom's visual environment can affect how much children learn" (Fisher, 2014).

So, keep this in mind:
- no extra personal décor if you can help it
- you don't need a theme, especially if this theme will unnecessarily bring visual overload to your students
- don't add something that doesn't serve your students. that is why you need to take everything down before putting only what is necessary on walls
- **less** in more
- too much on walls leads to cognitive and sensory load

Decoration

"Research… has shown the ability of interior design elements to evoke a positive or negative emotional response in people. These findings open the door to design spaces that consciously manipulate decorative elements with the goal of encouraging creativity, peace, and happiness." Chloe Taylor

Bring decoration to a minimum. Learning spaces should serve students. Function comes before cuteness, especially if the last one takes unnecessary space. I know that we, as teachers, have so many things we want to display, such as gifts from our students, all the cute frames, and pencil holders! The problem is that all this adds up and takes valuable space, space that can be empty! If you can't take everything down at once to start adding after having empty spaces, no worries! You can take a different approach, take one thing out of sight each day!

Students' stuff vs. teacher's stuff

"Material things are delightful, but they're not important." - Richard Branson

Finding the balance between having less of your stuff and more of your students' stuff displayed in the classroom is totally up to your judgment! I am not referring to your teacher's edition textbooks or manipulatives. I am referring to your personal stuff in the classroom, like your own décor and things that don't reflect your students' learning experience.

I am inviting you to look around in your classroom and decide what is represented more, your style, or your students' learning experience? Of course, we can have our personal things! But, the key is to find your own version of balance! You know your students and you also know how to represent them best in your classroom space!

We love our students' gifts, letters, and things that bring sweet memories. It is hard to put away those things. You can dedicate a space to display all this, instead of having it sprinkled around the classroom. Do what is best for you and your students. They love seeing what is important to you. They like knowing more about you through family pictures and gifts by them and former students!

Declutter, declutter, declutter!

"Owning less is better than organizing more." — Joshua Becker

Declutter walls, corners, bookshelves, things in storage, books, papers, file cabinets, supplies, furniture, things on tops of bookshelves, and whatever is left, try to put them in bins, cabinets, or behind curtains. You don't need to see everything you need. You can assign places for it and access it the same way without displaying it all!

Bookshelves:

"Out of calmness comes clarity." — Trevor Carss

Try to have bookshelves by categories and avoid putting décor and more bins on the tops of bookshelves. Avoid piling up things on top of desks, tables, bookshelves, and cabinets. Leave these types of surfaces clear as much as possible, so your students can access what they need in a more efficient and effective way.

Storage:

"Some things cost way more when we keep them." — Neeraj Agnihotri

After you bring everything to a minimum, store everything labeled by categories. Leave out only the things that are extremely necessary to be used frequently! This is easier said than done! I know! But we can start little by little!

For storage, you can have a uniform system that works for you and your students. You can make it functional for you and your students by putting frequently used resources closer to their reach according to their age. Share your system with them and ask for their input! I have had many break troughs because of my students' suggestions!

Location habit

"Success depends a lot on where you put things!!!!"- James Clear

This quote sums it all up! Please, read it again, and again, and again! I love this quote so much. Dwell on each word for a few minutes so you can get inspired to do the following:

- Keep close to you the objects you need frequently.
- Leave them always in the same place.
- Take a look at your teacher's desk. Are there things on or by it that you don't use frequently? If so, store it or donate it!
- This applies to classroom design, desks, offices, laptop screens, apps, purses, etc.
- Keep a bit farther the things you use less frequently.
- Get out of sight (it will be best if you get rid of) the things you never use. Just let them go.
- Want to get rid of bad habits? Get out of sight or throw things that will trigger those habits.
- Do you want to take a walk each day? Put your walking shoes by the door.
- Want to read more before going to bed? Put books by your bed and leave your phone in another room.
- Declutter. Declutter. Declutter. You will be able to just see the things you need.

Physical location is KEY for the formation of good habits! By having a location for each habit, not only you will feel more efficient, but you will start acquiring better habits. Better habits mean being more successful at reaching your personal and professional goals!

Bring nature to the classroom

"We must teach our children to smell the earth, to taste the rain, to touch the wind, to see things grow, to hear the sunrise and nightfall – to care."
~ John Cleal

Bring your students to nature as much as possible, but if this is not possible, bring nature as much as possible to your learning space. Display plants, use rocks as manipulatives, or other natural objects that are safe for your students to play with! Nature objects are so much better than plastic ones!

Some things from nature that you can use are rocks, sticks, seeds, leaves, seashells, wood, plants, twigs, acorns, and pine cones!

Bring students to nature

"Encourage your child to have muddy, grassy, or sandy feet by the end of each day. That's the childhood they deserve." ~Penny Whitehouse

"Experiences in natural settings provide multiple benefits to young children, including increased physical activity, reduced obesity, improved concentration, and enhanced social skills," says Jacobi-Vessels, Jill L. (2013) in Discovering Nature: The Benefits of Teaching Outside of the Classroom. We want and need all these benefits! Children and nature are one of the perfect combinations in this world!

Ideas to bring nature to your classroom or your students to nature!
- replace manipulatives for nature objects
- display flowers and plants on each table
- do art or displays on bulletin boards using nature
- read and/or have a picnic outside

- get your students outdoors as much as possible
- identify different types of trees, flowers, and plants
- adopt a classroom pet, raise butterflies or frogs
- nature show and tell
- play natural sounds softly: rain, birds, jungle, falls, etc.
- use that microscope more often
- talk more about nature in your lectures
- show more nature objects in your slides
- tell stories that take place in nature
- plant a tree, plant seeds in pots
- measure rainfall, feed the birds
- construct bird feeders on your classroom window
- take pictures of small creatures
- invite your students to look up and down to observe nature
- silence walk, poetry walk
- collect bugs and nature objects
- plants herbs and create soil layers
- experience different textures in nature
- invite your students to pay attention to the "small wonders"
- play nature sounds as your students work
- go outside just to appreciate and breathe fresh air
- invite your students to touch nature objects with their eyes closed to appreciate and compare different textures in flowers, leaves, rocks, etc.

Lights

"Natural light consistently fosters innovation, as does the avoidance of disturbances from noise and extreme temperatures." - David Livermore

Play with lights. To calm your students' brains, you can turn some lights off and turn the string lights on or even lamps! Dim lights can effectively calm your students' brains!

Brain Tips for a Home Learning Space for you as a Teacher, your Child, and your Students

"Home is the nicest word there is." —Laura Ingalls Wilder

A learning space that engages/energizes your children's brains: In this room or corner, bring all your crafts supplies, art supplies, puzzles, exercise videos, bright posters, bright light, and everything you can think of to have an inviting corner for you and your child to come when they feel creative. So, when it is time for lunch or something else, you don't have to put everything away or push it to the side, thus interrupting what you were doing. If you dedicate a space for this, when you have to do something else, you can just leave it where it is and return when you feel you are ready to resume it!

Find a space at home where you can use it to energize-engage your little ones! This space must be separate from the focus and calm spaces!

In this big or small space have the following:
- Good flow so your children can easily and quickly get what they need to be creative.
- Space for movement, so you can provide a space to exercise and have different positions while working.
- Add bright colors in the form of posters, décor, etc.
- Have bright lights.
- Add a table so collaboration among siblings or children/adults can happen.
- Add a makerspace/workshop/mini lab and put all the supplies you find at home in those places, so your child/children can have as many things as possible to be creative!

A learning space to focus your children's brains: In this room, mini-place or corner, bring all the things you need to focus such as reading, working on school assignments, etc. Try to have this space empty, with good lighting and minimal distractions. By having it this way, this space is a continual invitation to keep learning, and it will be there when you need it! Make sure this place is free of major distractions, like TV, or other members of the family working on various projects!

Find a space **at home** where you can use it to **focus** your little ones! This space must be separate from the engaging and calm spaces!

In this big or small space have the following:

- Put the minimum décor on this space.
- Only put up on walls something your child needs to focus on, which will help him with whatever they are learning.
- Have a significant portion of white (space) on the wall and décor in general.
- In this space, you can have books available for reading.
- You can also have different sets of flashcards.

A learning space that calms your children's brains: In this corner, bring all the things that help relax, calm and reset your mind, such as dim lights, soft music, a comfy chair, podcasts, audio stories, sensory bins, coloring books, journals. You never know when you or your child can feel overwhelmed and need space and time to reset. Having this set space will be a continual invitation to relax, to be focused, or engaged again.

When you have this calm space available at home, you know that you have a safe space to go to at any time when your mind needs a break. Find an area **at home** where you can use it to **calm** your little ones! This space must be separate from the engaging and focus spaces! In this big or small space have the following:

- Try to have this space in an area where there is no distraction on walls.
- Try to have dim lights in this space.
- You might want to create a mini nook so your child can work on different calm activities such as sensory bins, drawing, coloring, journaling, reflection, audio stories, and natural objects.

Remember, for every story, there is a setting. For every experience, there is a place that makes it unique. Learning is the same. Learning happens in a learning space, even at home!

In closing… before you start planning your units, and your instruction, take care of your students' learning space. The classroom needs to be intentionally designed to meet your students' brain needs: engaging/energizing, focusing, and calming their brains.

Decorate your classroom thinking beyond a theme, beyond just being cute, beyond decorating it according to your style. I have done all these things until I realized that my classroom is not just my classroom. It is my students' learning space. When you decorate your classroom, please bring this reference book with you!

For a ready-to-use **classroom design template, including a checklist for a brain-friendly design** that engages, energized, focuses, and calms your students' brains, go to: https://yanina-s-school.thinkific.com/courses/brainfriendlyteacherbookresources

And now, we are ready to **design instruction** that engages/energizes, focuses, and calms our students' brains!

Chapter 4: Brain-friendly Instructional Strategies

"I cannot teach anybody anything; I can only make them think." Socrates

Just as we need our learning space (classroom) to engage/energize, focus, and calm our students' brains, we also need instructional strategies to do the same! You will see why and how now! Students spend many hours at school, and their brains can be overwhelmed if the instructional strategies are not balanced. Meaning, that if you use strategies all day or the whole lesson that require prime focus, your students will be cognitively exhausted. As teachers, we need to balance our instruction so we can:

- Energize-engage our students' brains
- Focus our students' brains
- Calm our students' brains

I do not go to a gym to exercise, but I have a couple of weights at home. I have learned from experience that I can't lift weights for too long without warming up. I have also learned that it is better to rest the muscles before another round of lifting weights. The same happens with learning! The Psychology of Learning tells us we can't ask our students to sustain attention for too long and without warming up. We also need to provide downtime before asking them for another round of mental heavy lifting!

We cannot expect our students to hold attention, engagement, and energy for seven hours a day. That is why we need to balance our instruction so our students can warm up, be able to sustain attention, and rest. When we do this, they can have these cycles many times a day without experiencing cognitive load. When students experience cognitive load, they are too exhausted to keep learning. They just zone out! Besides, students need to have downtime after learning a concept and skills, because this is exactly when the new or modified knowledge can go into their long-term memory!

Learning happens in the brain, and if we have our students' brain needs in mind when we teach, our instructional strategies will be more effective!

Instructional Strategies that ENERGIZE/ENGAGE the Brain

These strategies aim to engage and energize students, hook their attention, and alert their brains. These strategies are used generally when students need to tackle multi-step, complex, and not-so-fun concepts.

"Student engagement refers to the degree of attention, curiosity, interest, optimism, and passion that students show when they are learning or being taught," says the fabulous Ed Glossary Reform website (2016). They also say that we teachers need to appeal not only to our students' intellectual engagement, but to their emotional, behavioral, physical, social, and cultural engagement as well.

Educational neuroscience expert Dr. David Sousa says, "student engagement can be defined as "the amount of attention, interest, curiosity, and positive emotional connections that students have when they are learning, whether in the classroom or on their own" (2016, p. 17). This helps students be intrinsically motivated to learn in class, achieve their learning goals, participate, and not give up when they encounter cognitive difficulties.

The following instructional strategies are high energy, and they help students be engaged and ready to absorb the concept that otherwise would be harder to do. The following are some examples of instructional strategies that engage/energize the brain at the beginning and throughout each class session!

List of instructional strategies, ideas, and activities that energize and engage your students' brains:

- Accountable talk
- Anchor activities
- Appointment clocks
- Ask constructed response questions like, which did…? Which can…? Which would? Why did…?
- Assessment-based instructional strategies
- Blogging
- Bring objects as writing prompts
- Brochure making
- Card recall
- Case studies
- Chatty room, ask kids to go to different stations to chat about questions posted on the walls.
- Class discussion using "real talk"
- Classroom transformation
- Comics
- Concept mapping
- Concrete-representational-abstract sequence of instruction
- Conferencing

- Cooperative learning
- Coordinate a live video with an organization, another classroom, author, professional, etc.
- Corner call
- Create a blog
- Create a mission for students to work on
- Create a movie trailer
- Create a podcast
- Create a poem
- Create a portfolio
- Create a song
- Create lists
- Create questions
- Create time capsules
- Crumple and shoot
- Current events conversation
- Debate
- Design thinking
- Differentiate content
- Differentiate process
- Differentiate product
- Differentiated learning environment
- Direct instruction (yes, it can be engaging!)
- Discovery/inquiry-based learning
- Double-entry journal
- Drama
- Draw a calculator on the floor so students can jump on the numbers to show the answer
- Dual coding, combining words and visuals
- Dynamic assessment
- Effective questioning
- Escape rooms
- Exit tickets
- Experiential learning

Brain-friendly Instructional Strategies

- Experiment
- Explicit teacher modeling
- Field experience
- Field study
- Field trip
- Flexible grouping of students
- Flexible/strategic grouping
- Flipped classrooms
- Gallery walk
- Gamification
- Giant calculator. Put tape on the floor forming the shapes of numbers where students can step on to answer questions
- Graffiti wall
- Guest speakers
- Hand signals
- Hands-on learning
- Heads together
- Hexagonal thinking
- Host a living museum or wax museum
- Humor in lessons
- Humor in slides
- Humor on posters
- Humor in instructions
- Humor on tests
- In your lessons or when your students teach, make sure the following elements are present: images, graphs, pictographs, podcast clips, sound effects, short video lessons, news, movie, and television show clips.
- Individualized instruction
- Infographic
- Inquiry-based learning
- Instructional conversations
- Instructional games
- Interactive learning walls

- Interview students
- Interview teachers
- Jeopardy
- Jigsaw
- Kagan quiz
- Learning centers
- Learning coach
- Literature centers
- Make a board game
- Make a commercial
- Mastery learning
- Math centers
- Mini white boards
- Minute papers
- Model thinking
- Modeling
- Modeling by teachers and students
- Music and songs
- Nature-based learning or some elements from it
- Number talks
- Offer choice
- Open-ended tasks
- Origami
- Panel/expert
- Peer review
- Peer teaching
- Peer interview
- Peer testing
- Pictionary
- Picture talk
- Planned discovery
- Play bingo
- Play charades
- Play hot potato

Brain-friendly Instructional Strategies

- Play Pictionary
- Play thumbs up – thumbs down
- Play trivia
- Play-based learning or some elements from it
- Plot map
- Problem-based learning
- Project-based learning
- Question choices
- Race-to-the-board games
- Rate it
- Read-aloud
- Reader's theater
- Reading & writing across the curriculum
- Realia: use of objects from real life used in classroom instruction
- Reciprocal teaching
- Response cards
- Response notebooks
- Role play
- Science centers
- Scoot
- Scrapbook
- Show and tell
- Show commercials
- Simulations
- Social studies centers
- Socratic seminar
- Sports-based learning or some elements from it
- Stem-based learning or some elements from it
- Sticking note graph
- Sticky notes
- Story telling round-robin
- Storyboards
- Strategies for fluency and speed

- Structured peer tutoring
- Student-created anchor charts
- Student-created questions
- Student-created games
- Student-created lectures
- Student-created tests
- Student-created comprehension questions
- Students teaching teachers
- Talk like an expert
- Task cards
- Teach concepts/skills within an authentic context
- Teaching metacognitive strategies
- Tell a riddle
- Think-aloud for students
- Think-pair-share
- Think-tac-toe
- Tiered activities
- Tiered rubrics
- Time capsule
- Timeline
- Trade cards
- Treasure hunt
- Use Jenga by putting tasks, problems, and basic operations problems on each piece.
- Use objects from nature as manipulatives
- Use of comic strips
- Use of dice
- Use of makerspace
- Use of mini-whiteboards
- Use of mini-whiteboards
- Use of real maps
- Use of stem lab
- Use online mind maps
- Use qr codes

- Use relevant physical objects when teaching math skills
- Use the following polls: Socratic, Google forms, Monkey Survey, and Poll Everywhere.
- Virtual field trip
- Vlogging
- Walk museum
- Wanted poster
- Watching a clip
- What is missing from the sentence, the story, the picture sequence cards, etc.?
- Word wall

Instructional Strategies that FOCUS the Brain

You and I know that we need our students to focus in order to tackle complex tasks, such as reading comprehension questions, multi-step problems, and application of learning, just to name a few. We can't ask our students to sustain uninterrupted focus for seven hours. That is why we need to have a balance and provide the time and space for our students to focus when they really need to maintain attention on learning something new, understanding a complex problem, and for many things that you know they can't do unless they focus! Focus is what helps students start, continue, and finish an assignment or project. Make sure you ask for focus for only certain assignments. We can't ask our students to maintain sustained attention for long!

The following instructional strategies, ideas, and activities require your students to focus. First, we need to provide students with time, space, and opportunities to focus. This is a crucial skill for cognitive and procedural tasks. These strategies require that you give your students the time and space to think. The concepts and skills that require focus are things your students need to understand in order to apply them in real life or solve even bigger problems.

Instructional Strategies that require FOCUS:

- Act as a resource
- Adapt
- Agendas
- Analysis
- Anchor activities
- Anticipation guides
- Application
- Appraise
- Arrange
- Art
- Ask & answer questions
- Assemble
- Assume
- Audio stories
- Author's point of view
- Award something or someone and why
- Brain dumps
- Break down
- Categorize
- Cause and effect
- Character traits
- Choose a sound to represent characters, emotions, actions, etc.
- Close reading
- Clues
- Clues to visualize a place
- Coming up with mnemonics
- Compare and contrast
- Comparison matrix
- Complete a decision-making matrix
- Concept attainment
- Concept maps
- Confirm predictions

- Consider author/illustrator intentions
- Consistent, 'low-threat' assessment
- Context clues
- Convergent and divergent thinking
- Cooperative learning cues, questions & advance organizers
- Correlate
- Create a list of criteria for judging
- Create rules
- Criticize a clip
- Criticize an article
- Criticize a book
- Debate
- Design
- Develop new "laws"
- Developing high expectations for each student
- Dialogue
- Different cover
- Different ending
- Different title
- Display essential questions
- Display goals
- Disprove and give reasons
- Dispute
- Dissect
- Document based-questions
- Doing art
- Doodling
- Drawing conclusions
- Dual coding
- Elaborate explanations starting with the word "because"
- Elaboration
- Elaboration, explain and describe ideas with many details
- Establish purpose
- Estimate

- Examine illustrations
- Fact and opinion
- Feedback
- Figurative language
- Find the theme
- Finding a long-term task demand stage of humor
- Flyers
- Forecast
- Form a panel
- Formative assessment process
- Generating and testing hypotheses
- Give out handouts in advance to promote anticipation
- Grade as you go
- Graphic organizers
- Guide creation
- Hexagonal thinking
- Higher-level questioning learning
- Homework & practice
- Identify change in feelings
- Identify feelings
- Identifying similarities and differences
- Imagination
- Independence stages
- Inspect
- Integration of content areas
- Interactive notebooks
- Interleaving, switching between ideas while learners study
- Interview
- Invent a machine
- Inventory your student's interests
- Judge
- KWL charts
- Learning contracts
- List

Brain-friendly Instructional Strategies

- Main ideas and details
- Make a family tree from the story
- Make/design a flowchart
- Making inferences
- Making predictions
- Menus
- Metacognition
- Metaphors and similes
- Multi-step problems
- Note-taking
- Notice structure
- Peer-teaching
- Personification
- Plan an itinerary
- Point out
- Post on social media or pretend to post
- Predictions
- Prepare a case
- Preview
- Prior knowledge
- Prioritize
- Probe
- Probe
- Problem and solution
- Promoting student metacognition
- Provide opportunities for student practice
- Provide time and space for your students to practice "self-explanation."
- Providing clear and effective learning feedback
- Puzzles
- Question-answer relationship
- Questions the author
- Recognize hidden meanings
- Recommendation

- References comments
- Reflection
- Reinforcing effort/providing recognition
- Relevance – why?
- Repetition
- Response notebooks
- Retelling
- Retrieval practice, practice bringing information to mind without the help of materials.
- Retrieval strategies
- Retrieving practices
- Review a book
- Reviewing
- Rewards-based on a specific performance standard
- Scaffolding instruction
- Seek patterns
- Self-explaining
- Sell an idea
- Sensory words
- Sequence
- Setting goals or objectives
- Setting objectives
- Simplify
- Social justice writing, reading, and conversations
- Space practice, space out studying over time
- Stick emojis on the text according to their emotions or yours
- Story-telling
- Structured academic controversy
- Student goal setting
- Student self-assessment
- Subdivide
- Summarizing and note-taking
- Suppose
- Survey

- Symbolism
- Talking and writing about "aha" or "wow" moments
- Targeted feedback
- Teacher clarity (learning goals, expectations, content delivery, assessment results, etc.)
- Test for connections
- Text connection
- Text to self
- Text to text
- Text to world
- Textual support
- The directed reading-thinking activity
- The theme, message, and lesson
- Theorize
- Thinking, questioning, epiphany
- Transitions in stories
- Uncover
- Understanding
- Why. Ask students "why" questions to you or their classmates.
- Word choice
- Word problems
- Words acting like pictures
- Words that paint pictures
- Words' meaning
- Write a letter to an author
- Write a letter to an illustrator
- Write a letter to an expert
- Write a letter to an essential worker
- Write a letter to the Mayor
- Write a letter to someone in the government
- Write a letter to the Principal
- Write a letter to the teacher
- Write a letter to a family member
- Writing assignments such as stories, reports, journals, etc.

Instructional Strategies that CALM the Brain

Let's go back to the gym analogy! Our muscles need to rest after strengthening them. The same needs to happen with our students' cognition strengthening. We need to provide the time and space for our students to calm their brains so they can rest from their cognition workout. When we do this, we give our students the opportunity to experience something even more important than resting and that is the **consolidation** of what they just learned. Let me share a little secret with you. I am fascinated with the process and gift of consolidation of learning!

If we as teachers don't provide time and space for our students to consolidate learning, when will their brains work on bringing what they learned to their long-term memory? When our students rest, sleep, or just have a downtime, their brains start organizing and bringing what they just learned to a place where that information can be retrieved again! AMAZING! We need to calm our students' brains before asking them to go to the next round of engaging/energizing and focusing activities. Before we ask them to learn something else or engage in another cognitive task, resting needs to happen. Otherwise, they will go through cognitive overload, and they will just turn off!

"When the brain is no longer actively engaged in learning, the information can be rapidly processed and consolidated. When you then sit down and relax, the brain rapidly repeats the neural sequence that was built up while walking, and eventually sends it to the cerebral cortex for final consolidation" say Henche and Sjogren (2021).

The following strategies can be used at the end of the day or a lesson, so students can have time to reset in order to be able to engage and focus again for the next class or lesson. These strategies help students, too, settle new learning **and** organize what was learned into their long-term memory.

Instructional Strategies that CALM our students' brains:

- Audio lessons
- Brain dumps
- Brain breaks
- Collages
- Coloring
- Connecting dots
- Craft
- Designing posters
- Diaries
- Free study time
- Independent study
- Journaling
- Listening to music
- Listening to podcasts
- Note-taking
- Painting
- Puzzles
- Reading
- Read-to-me books
- Reflection
- Response to clips
- Response to lecture
- Response to texts
- Take a trip to nature
- Talk to a trusted adult
- Talk to a friend
- Talk to a classmate
- Use of clay
- Use of a makerspace
- Use of a calm space
- Use of a stem lab
- Visit the library

- Walk outside
- Word search
- Working in the calm space
- Write a letters
- Write a song
- Write a poem
- Write a letter
- Write a reflection
- Write anything that comes to mind after the lesson

Ask your students for ideas. The way each student can calm their minds might be different than their classmates. Some might prefer to listen to music, while others will prefer to enjoy silence. Do your best to accommodate those students who really need to rest before going on to the next class, activity, or task!

For ready-to-use instructional strategies, go to:
https://yanina-s-school.thinkific.com/courses/brainfriendlyteacherbookresources

At the Brain-friendly Teacher Academy & Book Resources, you will also find:

- ready-to-use instructional resources for a meaningful and lasting learning experience
- a master class taught by me
- templates for annual, unit, and daily lesson plans

Enjoy!!!
https://yanina-s-school.thinkific.com/courses/brainfriendlyteacherbookresources

Chapter 5: Practical Instructional Strategies to Create Lasting Learning

"Live as if you were to die tomorrow. Learn as if you were to live forever."
Mahatma Gandhi

Lasting learning is when we have knowledge and information in our long-term memory. There are some things that we can remember for a long time. In my case, these are the things I will remember forever: the first time I saw my babies, the day my family and I got three puppies, and the day I got my first job as a teacher.

Before information gets to long-term memory though, it is located in short-term memory. Short-term memory is the capacity to store a small amount of information for a short period of time. Short-term memory allows you to remember just a few things for just a few seconds. What you do with that information is managed by the working memory. In other words, working memory is what you do with the information of your short-term memory. When you perform a task, your working memory uses the information from your short-term memory.

Your students need to remember information for a few seconds (short-term memory) to work on an assignment (working memory) you have given them. Short memory only lasts a few seconds, though, so don't give too many directions at the same time!!!

As teachers, we not only need to understand how short-term and working memory work, but we also need to understand how we can bring information to long-term memory. Why? We need and want our students to remember what we teach, what they learn, and read for more than a few seconds, right?

Besides, **"true learning only takes place when information has been moved from working memory into long-term memory"** (Oakley and Schewe, 2021, pg. 42). We, educators, must do something with the information to ensure it gets stored where it needs to be so it can be retrieved whenever needed!

Let me take a break here to encourage you to explain to your students how their brains work and how they need to help their brains bring the information they need to their long-term memory! This is a conversation about how learning works, not just brain parts and functions. When they understand how learning works and why teachers use some particular strategies, they will not only do better on assignments and assessments, but they will take ownership of their own learning experience. More importantly, **true learning** will happen **and stick** to help them in their real life! They need to know this, no matter what their age is! But, of course, you need to use the words that will better resonate with them, but students at any age should be aware of what their brains like and need so they can have a meaningful and lasting learning experience!

And now to the practical strategies to bring knowledge, concepts, and skills to your students' long-term memory! This is how you can help your students create lasting learning!

These are research-based instructional strategies, practical tips, and ideas to help you bring what you teach to your student's long-term memory. I am sure you have heard of them already. These strategies are very simple and easy to implement, and sometimes, because they are simple, we tend to underestimate their power when used frequently and intentionally! So, I am inviting you to take them even more seriously! If you don't have your highlighter and your notebook already, now is the time!!!

This chapter has a lot of strategies, so leave this book on your desk or by your teacher planner at all times so you can get ideas to teach your next annual, unit, or daily lesson plans! Treat this book as a reference book! Bring all the sticky notes and bookmarks!

But let's see first why knowing about long-term memory is crucial in the process of teaching and learning!

Long-term memory is the ability to both store and recall information for later use. The information that is long-term memory can store information forever. We can transfer information to long-term memory by repeating, using, and retrieving it.

As teachers, we want students to bring knowledge and skills **from short-term memory**, the "capacity to recall a small amount of information from a recent time period" **to long-term memory**, the "capacity to recall memories from a long time ago" (Huizen, 2021).

We want our students to remember important facts, knowledge, and skills for a long-time, especially the information they need to solve problems and as background knowledge in order to understand more complex information. As teachers, it is very helpful to know that long-term memory can be explicit and implicit. The explicit can be episodic (events) or semantic (knowledge and concepts), and the implicit can be procedural (skills) and emotional conditioning.

Caine, Caine, McCLintic, Kimiex (2009, pg. 204) lists the types of memories more simply:

- "Declarative memory - memory for facts
- Procedural memory - memory for skill and procedures
- Episodic memory - memory of events in one's life
- Semantic memory - memory for the meaning of words
- Emotional memory - memory involving emotions."

We need to be intentional about how we teach or what tools we use to help our students remember events, concepts, and skills. Especially if these things are needed to solve problems, apply them to the real world, and understand other events, concepts, and skills.

The following strategies, ideas, and tips will help you bring concepts and skills to your students' long-term memory! But first, let's take a look at the VITAL CYCLE for true learning!

The learning cycle

"Try to learn something about everything and everything about something."
- Thomas Huxley

Encoding refers to the initial experience of perceiving, encountering, and absorbing new information inside our students' brains. It is when you initially teach something new or add more information to something previously learned. In this stage, it is important to engage/energize the brain with emotions, movement, music, songs, novelty, etc. Our students' brains don't encode everything we see, hear, etc. They decide what we pay attention to! So, make it relevant from the beginning.

Consolidation: every experience and knowledge we absorb changes our brains. Our students' brains change during encoding and consolidation! After our students learn something new (encoding), their brains start consolidating that information. Their brains start reorganizing that information and associating it with other things they learned or experienced before. They start making sense of it. During this process, students' brains give meaning to what they learned and make connections to prior knowledge stored in their long-term memory. This is why it is important to help your students in this process by using graphic organizers, concept maps, etc. so the new information can make sense, get organized, and ultimately, *consolidated*. For this to happen, provide the time and space to focus in the classroom.

Retrieval: information that can't be retrieved is useless. Retrieval is when we ask our students to bring back something that they have learned or experienced before. For students to be able to retrieve tomorrow, next week, next month, or next year; they need to retrieve it by repeating the information or content without looking at their textbooks. Re-reading doesn't work! Before we ask our students to retrieve, we need to make that encoding and consolidation make sense for our students. These are cognitive skills we can't externally perform for our students. Their brains do it. We can certainly help our students in a way, but ultimately it is their brains that take care of it! Make sure you have time for retrieval strategies in your classroom, so the learning cycle can be complete, meaningful, and lasting!

There are so many amazing and simple retrieval strategies, such as:
- brain dumps
- peer teaching
- spacing and interleaving
- oral and written reviews or reflections
- and so many more you will read in this book.

Music

Music touches us emotionally, where words alone can't. – Johnny Depp

Music is one of the most powerful things in the universe! Music is medicine for the mind! According to a study at Johns Hopkins Medicine (2021), music improves mood, mental alertness, and memory while reducing stress and anxiety. We need all this in our classrooms! There are countless benefits to listening to and creating music. Music helps students remember information **and create new memories**! So powerful!

I am sure you have used songs to learn things for yourself or to teach your students multiplication facts, parts of plants, etc.! I bet you start singing a song when a student is stuck with a problem. Then, your student finishes the song and solves the problem! Music is powerful. Powerful not only to store and retrieve concepts, facts, and skills from memory, but for many other things in your classroom!

Ways you can use music in your classroom:

- Welcome and dismiss students with music
- Use it for transitions
- Use music to cue different moods: energetic, calm, suspense, etc.
- To memorize facts
- To memorize multiplication facts, parts of the speech, states, etc.
- Class timer.
- To teach phonics, pronunciation, and vocabulary.
- To go back in time when you teach a history lesson.
- For cool and surprising sound effects.
- To retell a story.
- Attach it to a classroom management technique.

- Just to appreciate different styles of music and artists.
- To talk about how we can healthily express feelings.
- To set the tone for games.
- To learn specific concepts. www.flocabulary.com has amazing videos for this!
- To create the atmosphere needed for a specific task, like suspense, energy, and concentration.
- For brain breaks.
- To have a very soft background, if students are reading about a jungle, you can play jungle sounds very softly in the background or rain.
- To make a triumphal entrance.
- To set the tone for the beginning of a new unit.
- To set the tone for the end of a unit or story.
- To have as a background as they color or paint.

Movement

"Movement is the most transformative thing we can do for our brains"
- Wendy Suzuki

Every time we think of a school setting or learning, we visualize students sitting at their desks. Why is this? We got used to seeing students sitting all day while learning. It really doesn't have to be this way. Especially with all we know about the power of moving **while and between** learning sessions! Movement helps students **store, consolidate, and retrieve** information! Imagine!!!

Jensen, the author of "Teaching with the Brain in Mind " reminds us that "when we keep students active, we keep their energy levels up and provide their brains with oxygen-rich blood needed for highest performance" (pg. 66). Whenever students move in class, they are immediately engaged, awake, and alert!

In her famous TED Talk about Movement, Dr. Wendy Suzuki also shares the benefits of movement in our brains:

- Better mood
- Increased energy
- Better attention
- Improved memory, short and long term
- Increase in brain mass

Ideas to use movement in the classroom:

- Morning routine
- Movement that accompanies music
- Flexible seating or not in your classroom, you can still provide opportunities to move. Even if you have desks for all your students, you can have a few standing desks and some empty areas where students can work or read on the floor.
- Movement for vocabulary: instead of writing a sentence on paper, they can act the meaning.
- Plays
- Sketches
- Students can move around to demonstrate concepts of just working in groups in science class.
- Remember that your classroom should be functional. This would make it easier to move furniture around so your students can move around too!
- Students can work on mnemonics by using their bodies to form letters or words.
- Physical breaks, instead of or besides passive brain breaks
- Physical representations of numbers, rules, concepts, skills
- Representation of science concepts, such as rotation of Earth
- Representation of math concepts: triangles, parallelograms, etc.
- Representations of parts of an essay: hook, transitions, etc.

Emotions

"The best and most beautiful things in the world cannot be seen or even touched. They must be felt with the heart" — Helen Keller.

Every time you had an emotional-charged (good or bad) experience, you can tell others exactly what happened at every minute of that event. This happens because emotionally charged situations create lasting memories in our brains.

When you teach a lesson or read a book, talk about the emotions and feelings that those words create in your students' minds. You can also put yourself and your students in the shoes:

- of those who fought for good causes
- of those who discovered and invented amazing things that have changed our lives
- of those who paid big prices for their beliefs

Help them think about the emotions that scientists, heroes, children, people from different countries and cultures, presidents, persecuted people, etc., might have felt during the moments they were making history without knowing.

Imagination

"The man who has no imagination has no wings." - Muhammad Ali.

Imagination is the ability of your mind to create images, sensations, and ideas without receiving any help from your senses. This is just done by your mind! Incredible, right? This is an amazing skill that we can use to help our students invent things, write better... the possibilities are endless, just like their imagination!

Students' creativity is fueled by their imagination. This is a fantastic skill that we can use to help students in their learning process! "Imagination allows us to think of things that aren't real or around us at any given time, while creativity allows us to do something meaningful with our imaginations" (Aubrey Jones, 2019).

I know you have a lot to cover each class and that you barely have a minute for transitions between classes! But, if you can try to provide the time and space for students to use their imagination for their creative endeavors, you will see surprising results over time! Now, students not only need to absorb information but also be creative with the use of that information. That way, they can use what they learn in real projects to solve real problems. And for this to happen, students need to have time and space to use their imagination.

Do this for me: look around wherever you are now. Everything you see now was created by someone. And that creation happened after that person imagined it first! This book too! Think about it! Now **imagine** giving the space and time to your students so they can use their **imagination**. Now **imagine** what they could do with their **imagination**!!!

This is how you can foster imagination in your classroom:

- Ask unusual questions.
- Ask "Why," "How," and "What if?"
- Invite them to imagine a different ending.
- Have them create prototypes.
- Promote entrepreneurship.
- Facilitate a creative/imagination hour per week or a few minutes per day
- Invite them to make predictions before reading a book.
- Use analogies

- Use metaphors.
- Anticipate difficulties and solutions.
- Say something like this: "If you lived in this book… what would you…? If you lived in Ancient Egypt… If you were a…
- Promote curiosity!
- Display inspirational quotes about imagination.
- Read stories about inventors, authors, musicians, artists, architects, engineers, carpenters, etc.
- Allow pretend play.
- Host a Genius Hour each week!
- Implement Project-based Learning!

Mnemonics

"A mnemonic is an instructional strategy designed to help students improve their memory of important information." adlit.org

Mnemonic devices are memory techniques that help students' brains encode and recall important information more effectively. It's a simple shortcut that helps them associate the information we want to remember with an image, a sentence, or a word. Mnemonic devices started in Greek, and now we have many types! Mnemonics use music, names, expression/word, model, ode/rhyme, note organization, image, connection, and spelling.

The following are the types of mnemonics your students can use to bring important knowledge to their long-term memory. The best part of this strategy is that your students can come up with their own ways of using it to remember important information. The process itself of coming up with a mnemonic is already playing a massive role in sticking the information. After the mnemonic is created, it needs to be repeated frequently in order to stick even more permanently.

These are types of mnemonics you can use with your students:

- Musical Mnemonics, change lyrics with the information you need to memorize.
- Keywords mnemonics, for each concept, find a word, and that will remind you of the rest.
- Rhymes, write your info in the form of a poem and you will see how powerful that is!
- Acronyms, remember only the first letter of each word, a sentence or paragraph that will cue you for the rest.
- Chunking, retain only brief parts of each section you need to memorize. Each part will remind you of the piece of information you need to retain.
- Letters and words combined, add numbers to words, so you can connect that info with quantity.
- Alliterations mnemonics.
- Visual mnemonics or image connections.
- Note organization.
- Spelling mnemonics.
- Making connections, connecting the information to emotions, lived experiences, places, people, etc.
- Have students come up with their own types of mnemonics.
- The LOCI method is about imagining a place that is very familiar to you, like your house. Then, you associate a word, term, definition, or idea to each part of the house. If your students need to explain something in a specific order, they need to associate the order of the information to be memorized with the order in which they see the rooms or things in their house as they get in!

Even though mnemonics are not a higher-order thinking skill, they surely can help students recall information and facts that will be used in higher-order thinking activities!

Story-telling

"Storytelling is the most powerful way to put ideas into the world."
— Robert McKee

"When you want to motivate, persuade, or be remembered, start with a story of human struggle and eventual triumph. It will capture people's hearts – by first attracting their brains" (Zak, 2014).

This is why you should use stories when teaching something you want your students to remember! Anand, in his article "The Neuroscience: Why Your Brain Loves Good Storytelling" wrote:

- "Stories activate multiple senses in the brain; motor, auditory, olfactory, somatosensory, and visual."
- When students listen to stories, they can imagine what they are hearing. Each student imagines the scenes and characters in a different way. While students listen to stories, they can draw or doodle what they imagine. Then, they can share what they drew with their classmates. They will see firsthand how each of one them imagines and understands stories differently!
- Stories help students remember concepts and information more effectively since they associate emotions and senses with them.
- Students identify with characters from stories
- When students listen to stories, they can use the same elements and sequences when they write their own stories.
- Storytelling is one of the most powerful techniques we have as humans to communicate, motivate, and inspire to action.
- Cognitive science has long recognized narrative as a basic organizing principle of memory.

Ways you can start sharing stories in the classroom!

- Share your own story or experiences.
- Use a story to introduce a new topic.
- Use a story to illustrate a new concept.
- Use a true story, even if it is not your own.
- Inspire to take action with stories.
- Invite to reflect, pause, and reset with stories.
- Go back in time with stories.
- Use parables, illustrations, a silly story, fictional story for your lesson.
- Stories can and should be told in math too! Especially in math!

Relevance

*"To bring relevance to people,
you have to be able to speak their language effectively"* — *Sunday Adelaja*

"Relevance is the perception that something is interesting **and** worth knowing" (Roberson, 2013). Before our students ask us, "Why are we even learning this?" or "when am I going to use this?" We can start the lesson by explaining the **why** behind it. We can give concrete examples of how the lesson is **relatable and useful** now and in the future!

We know we need to share with our students the relevance of each lesson, concept, or skill. But, many times we jump into the lesson because time is precious! I encourage you to add a space into your lesson plans to write a few words about the relevance of the lesson to be shared with your students. Remember to tell them how that can be related to them and how they can use it now and in the future. If you can talk more about the uses of the near future than the distant future, bonus points!

"Relevant, meaningful activities that both engage students emotionally and **connect with what they already know** are what help build neural connections and long-term memory storage" (Briggs, 2014). We can add a third element now to relevance, and that is to connect the new concept to a concept they already know! So relevance is about sharing with our students how that new concept is relatable, how that concept can be used now and in the future, and how the concept is an extension of what they already know!

Ideas to bring relevance to your students

- Utilize real-world problems for classroom activities
- Plan a field trip
- Connect to what students know
- Invite a guest speaker
- Use primary source documents
- Observe the world around you
- Ask older students to "be the expert"
- Re-vamp word problems
- Use the news
- Make assignments look "real world"
- Show a documentary
- Use simulations
- Student input
- "publish" student work for the larger community
- Use connect to self, connect to other texts, connect to the world
- Start with a real-world problem in mind
- Bring an expert to the classroom
- Host a career-day
- Provide an audience to your students
- Write for a kid's magazine
- Write for a local newsletter
- Write for your school/class newsletter

Novelty

"Life begins at the end of your comfort zone." Neale Donald Walsch

"The brain craves novel experiences and processes them with high priority" (Schomaker & Meeter, 2014). High priority! Did you catch that? And there is even more! "The brain/mind is designed to immediately respond to novelty" (Caine, Caine, McClintic, Klimek, 2009, pg. 217). This happens to you, too. Doesn't your brain wake up or get more alert when something unexpected happens, or when you receive a surprise? I bet you can remember everything from that experience!

And there is, even more, to say about novelty! "Novelty has a wide range of effects on cognition; **improving perception and action, increasing motivation, eliciting exploratory behavior, and promoting learning**" (Schomaker and Meeter, 2015). It also "improves memory" (Cooper, 2013). The thing with novelty and the classroom is that if we do the same kind of surprises for our students, it is not a novelty anymore. Novelty doesn't have to come in the form of huge surprises. It can be just a little something that is different in the classroom routine!

Ideas to bring novelty and, therefore, "attention and retention" to the classroom:

- Welcome your students wearing a silly thing.
- Change your voice as you greet your students.
- Transform your classroom according to the topic you will teach.
- Wear something very unusual and that goes with the lesson.
- Include gamification.
- Do escape rooms.
- Try a never-done approach and see what happens.

- Provide multi-sensory experiences.
- Welcome them with a special song.
- Wear a hat.
- Wear a gig.
- Act differently or as a character from a book!

Reading

"Books are the quietest and most constant of friends; they are the most accessible and wisest of counselors, and the most patient of teachers." — Charles W. Eliot

Reading is not just about getting information in our brains, it is about actually changing it! Reading does so much for our brains. These are just a few benefits of reading!

- Reading builds up our ability to focus and grasp complex ideas.
- Reading rewires the brain.
- Reading about an experience is like you're living it yourself.
- Different reading styles create different brain patterns.
- Reading makes us more empathetic.
- We make images in our minds while reading.
- Reading relaxes and boosts vocabulary.
- Reading from a screen lacks spatial navigability, that is why paper books are better!
- "Reading ability in children is related to the growth of the brain's white matter tracts." (Reading and the Brain. Harvard Medical School. Gaab 2016)

Ideas to invite students to read, read, read!
- Ask students about their interests and check those books at the library.

- Dedicate the most beautiful, calm, attractive space in your classroom for reading.
- Have a day when they can read with flashlights under their desks.
- Ask them to bring a teddy bear as a reading buddy.
- Bring picture books no matter the age of the learners.
- Read stories aloud no matter the age of the learners.
- Get into the story, and bring all those emotions!!!
- Allow students to judge the book.
- Have them bring a page of the book alive!!
- Provide a listening station where they can listen to audiobooks.
- Come to school in a costume of a book character.
- Invite them to read to a younger student at your school.
- Invite authors.
- Use the gift of books as treats for meeting reading goals.
- Invite students to read to you, for fun!
- During reading time, read your favorite book as a teacher so students can see that reading is important and fun for you too!

Reviewing and retrieving

"Learning is a treasure that will follow its owner everywhere."
- Chinese Proverb

And now, some shocking news. Well, maybe not so shocking to teachers!!! German psychologist Hermann Ebbinghaus discovered that we quickly forget what we learn. He is famous for his **Forgetting Curve**. "Ebbinghaus discovered that without any reinforcement or connections to prior knowledge, information is quickly forgotten—roughly 56 percent in one hour, 66 percent after a day, and 75 percent after six days" (Terada, 2017).

Wow, this is pretty discouraging, but the good news is that we **can** do something about it!!!

We can use retrieval practices! Dr. Awargal, the amazing researcher on the power of retrieval practices in the classroom, says: "Retrieval practice boosts learning by pulling information out of students' heads, rather than cramming information into students' heads." We tend to think that most learning occurs during the initial encoding stage–when students get information "in" by re-reading, reviewing, and taking notes. However, in her book Powerful Teaching, one of the most robust findings from 100+ years of cognitive science research proves that a significant amount of learning occurs when students pull information "out" through retrieval practice.

The authors of another must-read book on the science of learning, "Make it Stick," say that "practice at retrieving new knowledge or skill from memory is a potent tool for learning and durable retention" (Brown, Roediger III, and Mc Daniel, 2014). We can apply retrieval practices not only for facts but also for problem-solving techniques and motor skills.

By doing this, we are bringing out of their brains what students have read and learned. These practices help students remember for much longer what they have learned, especially if we do this frequently. This is some amazing news, right?

Please, review frequently by using some of the following strategies!

- Bingo
- Brain dumps
- Collaborative review
- Combine text with images
- Escape rooms
- Family feud

- Flashcards
- Frequent practice tests
- Gamification
- Go outside to review using chalk
- Have students quiz each other in pairs with task cards, flashcards, or other test prep questions
- Headbands
- Hot seat
- I have, who has
- Interleaving: teach various concepts at the same time
- Jeopardy & Monopoly
- Peer-to-peer explanations
- Pictionary
- Review anchor charts
- Review organizers
- Review questions on a beach ball
- Scavenger hunt
- Self-explanation
- Spacing
- Spin the wheel
- Student-generated questions
- Students teaching the material
- Use checkers, trouble, battleship, or connect 4, Jenga blocks,
- Use interactive books
- Use QR codes

Spaced practice

*"Patience is not simply the ability to wait —
it's how we behave while we're waiting"* - Joyce Meyer

This practice boosts learning by pulling information out of our students' brains. Spacing is the practice of spreading lessons and retrieval opportunities over time, so learning is not crammed all at once. When you plan, try to set aside a time or a buffer to return and review content taught last week or last month. When the information is reviewed or frequently visited, the better the chance to be stored and retrieved from your students' long-term memory!

Feedback

"There is no failure. Only feedback." – Robert Allen

Our brains crave feedback, especially quick feedback while we are still working on something. This is known in the classroom as formative assessment. "Feedback is an essential part of the learning process" (Stenger, 2014).

Feedback is a crucial tool that teachers can use to commend what students are doing right, inform where they can improve, and point to what students are missing or getting wrong. This helps students to practice metacognition, improve, and reflect on their learning experience!

Feedback needs to be:
- Mostly positive
- Clear
- Specific
- Immediate
- Frequent
- Student-involved
- Student-goal oriented

Instead of telling your students what a good job they are doing, you can use these more specific phrases:

- I noticed how you didn't give up on writing a captivating hook for that paragraph!
- I saw how you kept on working on that subtraction across zeros until you got it right!
- I noticed how you kept improving the drawing of that flower!

"Pay attention"

> *"Attention is vitality. It connects you with others. It makes you eager. Stay eager." - Susan Sontag*

What kind of attention do we need or are referring to when we say, "Attention, please!" or use any other kind of attention getters? Do we need **sustaining, selective, alternating, or divided attention** from our students? Mazarin (2021) says that sustained attention is the ability to focus and concentrate for a few minutes, depending on the age and brain of your students.

When you are teaching a mini-lesson, lecturing, or explaining an important point, you do need **sustained attention** from your learners. But remember that sustained attention lasts about 12 minutes in a 6-year-old child, and it increases by 5 minutes each year until 30 minutes. Thirty minutes is about the longest a person can display **sustained attention**.

We can't require sustained attention constantly. If your task can be done with the other types of attention, go for it. But, if you really need, and we do, **sustained** attention, have in mind that the lessons, lectures, clips, and audios need to be short and sweet or with breaks in between sections of the lecture or lesson!

Attention is limited

"To pay attention, this is our endless and proper work."
— Mary Oliver

Sustained attention is very limited. So, if you are expecting your students to pay undivided attention to you for a long period of time, instead of undivided attention, you will get divided attention. You might also get selective attention and even alternating attention. Meaning, that they will just pay attention for a few minutes and wander off again. They simply can't sustain attention even if we ask them to keep paying attention!

If you are teaching online, in-person or hybrid, you have noticed that one thing is limited for sure! Even if students are in front of a stimulating screen, attention is limited. (If there is a way that you can reduce screen hours as a teacher or switch assignments to the on-paper option, please go for it!)

Include the following strategies at the beginning, in-between, and end of your lessons. Students need a break before paying sustained attention all over again! Remember the analogy about lifting weights at the gym or at home! We simply can't lift weights for long periods of time. We need warming up time and breaks in between the heavy lifting! Paying attention is a "heavy" cognitive skill!

- 3D projects
- Art
- Asking ungoogleable questions
- Audio stories
- Avoiding busywork
- Avoiding cognitive load
- Brain teasers
- Breathing exercises

- Calm down opportunities
- De-cluttered space
- Doing less
- Doodling
- Drawing
- Frequent breaks
- Games
- Hexagonal thinking
- Independent reading time
- Invitation to drink water
- Metacognition
- Mnemonics
- Movement
- Nature objects
- Note-taking
- Peer-teaching
- Puzzles
- Reflection journals
- Review games
- Songs
- Use of dim and bright lights
- Use of emotions
- Use of humor
- Use of imagination
- White and empty spaces in space, worksheets, and time
- Working in groups

and so many more brain-friendly, powerful and practical tips to make sure true learning is happening while attending to your students' brain needs. In fact, this book is full of those strategies. Strategies that are all about balancing instruction, so your students can energize/engage, focus, and calm their minds!

Let them daydream!

"Is daydreaming a distraction from work, or work a distraction from daydreaming?" -Marty Rubin.

We, teachers, think that our job description also includes, "Catch the daydreamers and ask them to come back to class!" If we are constantly calling out students who are daydreaming for a few minutes during class, we are forgetting that daydreaming is actually a natural brain need.

"The most common view of the human mind assumes that our normal way of thinking consists of concentrated focus upon immediate tasks at hand. But researchers have found that this is not the case. **Daydreaming** is **now** considered being the **normal state** of our minds" (Koch, 2013).

About daydreaming promotes:

- Critical thinking and intelligence
- Motivation
- Confidence
- Improved problem-solving
- Coping
- Creativity
- Concentration
- Connection to class material
- Increased empathy and emotional intelligence
- Improved self-knowledge

The tendency to daydream is a normal brain activity. Daydreaming helps us explore new ideas, promotes creativity, improves working memory, and gives the brain a break, which improves performance and productivity. Daydreamers are better problem solvers. "Daydreaming, like nighttime dreaming, consolidates learning" (Dave, 2020). As teachers, we need to provide a few minutes to daydreaming, so learners don't do it when they need to make use of sustained attention!

I am guilty of seeing a student daydreaming for a minute while reading a book, doing math, or writing answers on a paper and saying, "Let's go back to work!" But **what if** that student was:

- Having an AHA moment.
- Reflecting on what she/he was learning.
- Curious about the ending.
- Planning to ask questions.
- Making sense of what the student is learning.
- Connecting that info to her/his world.
- Planning to go home and do something about it.
- Encoding and consolidating learning.
- Taking a needed break from cognitive load.
- Thinking about some personal problems, worries, and plans.
- Getting some ideas to do later.
- Actually, who knows? They might just need a mental break to settle things in, reflect, plan to take action, or just wonder!

Most of the school day, learners need sustained attention and focus. We are there to teach them how to do that, but there are also times when we can be flexible and let them daydream for a few minutes! Their brains need it! We don't have to announce, though, "Time to daydream!" We can just be flexible if that happens to a student, especially if it is not interfering in their learning process at a time when attention has to be sustained. Sustained attention should not be too long, anyway... and daydreaming, either!

You know best how to be flexible in your classroom. You know how to maintain academic rigor while having in mind your students' brain needs!

Peer-teaching

"Better than a thousand days of diligent study is one day with a great teacher"
- Japanese Proverb

When students teach to their classmates, they:

- Tend to seek out key points and organize information into a coherent structure.
- Develop a deeper, longer, and lasting understanding of the material.
- Enhance learning by enabling them to take responsibility for reviewing, organizing, and consolidating existing knowledge and material.
- Improve confidence.
- Understand the material's basic structure.
- Fill in their gaps of understanding.

Teachers might have some valid excuses for not letting their students teach lessons once in a while, but the benefits are incredible!!!

- Students learn the material better because they have to explain it.
- Students practice presentation and leadership skills.
- Students gain independence. They don't have to do everything by themselves, without a teacher's guidance, but they definitely have the chance to rely on themselves to steer their learning and do what they see as necessary to master the material well enough to share with others.
- Students take approaches and ideas we wouldn't have ourselves.
- Students relate the content to students.
- Students need to organize the material to understand it and explain it.

- Classmates listen more to classmates and relate to the way they explain things.

This is how you can do it in your classroom:

- Model first
- Offer a template or written prompts
- Make groups small
- Don't make their lesson contingent on a prior lesson
- Help them see the learning objectives of the lesson they will be teaching
- Give ideas of what students can do to engage their classmates
- Teach them how to give feedback
- The primary objective of having students teach the class is that they learn the content through their own process of teaching

Making and Viewing Art

"Every child is an artist. The problem is how to remain an artist once we grow up." – Pablo Picasso

As soon as we mention "art" in schools, we immediately think of it as a separate class. But, this doesn't have to be this way. In the real world, art is integrated with design, engineering, architecture, math, science, technology, and language arts, you get the point. Art is everywhere! Wouldn't be nice to integrate art into our lessons as much as we can?

These are the benefits of making and viewing art:
- Attention to details about shape, form, color, texture, and other elements
- Making art is all about finding multiple solutions and answers to a task or a problem
- Being driven by imagination and daydreaming

- Realization that art is found in all areas, subjects, and fields
- Art can improve our quality of life
- Children naturally love art in all its forms
- Engagement of all the senses
- Dwelling in the appreciation of something new and beautiful
- Paying close attention to detail, textures, and style
- Connecting art to the real world
- Deep reflection
- Relieving of stress
- Encouragement of creative thinking
- Increasing brain plasticity
- Appreciation of people from the past
- Appreciation of diversity
- Viewing art increases empathy and tolerance
- Creation of different feelings, including love
- Increase thinking skills
- "The act of viewing art gives pleasure, much like falling in love" (Meg. H, 2018).

Try to use arts in all subjects. Students love art, but sometimes they don't make a connection or see art in math, art in social studies, art in science, and art in language arts. Check into STEAM projects. There is a myriad of ideas on how to use art in all areas!

Doodling

"Doodling, for me, is thinking and making at the same time." - Jon Burgerman

Have you ever found yourself doodling while listening or thinking? "Drawing with pencil, pen, or brush on paper isn't just for artists. For anyone who actively exercises the brain, doodling and drawing are ideal for making ideas tangible" (Heller 2015). "When you draw an object, the mind becomes deeply, intensely attentive," says the designer Milton

Glaser, an author of a 2008 monograph titled **Drawing is Thinking**.

Doodling not only provides relaxation, but attention, retention, and concentration. When students doodle while listening, they remain highly focused on what they are listening to. Doodlers create symbols in their brains and make ideas tangible. Doodling is essential for expressing spontaneous concepts and emotions.

Ways to use doodling in the classroom:

- As you tell a story, you can distribute a blank sheet of paper so your students can doodle as they listen to you. Some will do free doodling, others might draw squares and write the story in sequence, others will put the theme in the middle and arrows pointing at different scenes, and who knows what you might get from their doodling!
- Then, you can ask students to share their doodling with their neighbors
- Finally, you can conclude by pointing out that each learner paid attention to something different in the story and that we all learn differently according to our experiences, likes, and needs!
- You can have them listen to a podcast while they doodle.
- You can replace worksheets with doodling, where they have to doodle to evaluate a lesson, create a plan, do reading comprehension, explain science concepts, and so many more subjects, lessons, and learning experiences.
- They can doodle prototypes before making something.
- The opportunities to use doodling in the classroom are countless. Be creative.

Asking "why"

> *"The art and science of asking questions is the source of all knowledge"*
> -Thomas Berger

Students' questions show how they think, more than their answers! Students need to be invited to ask more questions! Give them time and space for students to ask and write down as many questions as they have, not only "why" questions, but any kind of questions they may have.

For students, the **why** is more important than the lesson.

- Remember to discuss the **why** of each one of your lessons! Be invested into that **why** yourself too!
- Make sure you are in the same boat as to **why** that lesson will help you as a teacher in real-life and your students as well!
- The **why** needs to come before the **what** and the **how**.

Taking notes

> *"When your heart speaks, take good notes."* - Judith Exner

Note-taking provides several benefits beyond the record of what was presented in a lecture or class activity. You can invite your students to take notes in their own way and depending on their age. These are some of the amazing benefits of note-taking:

- keeps your students alert
- avoids distraction
- engages your students' minds
- promotes active listening

- helps organize the information
- engages minds
- helps students condense and synthesize information
- requires cognition effort
- helps the organization of thoughts
- regulates and maintains attention
- uses working memory
- facilitates long-term memory retrieval
- requires visual-spatial processing
- requires auditory processing
- helps students focus and sustain attention
- facilitates analysis
- facilitates prediction
- facilitates planning
- facilitates sequencing
- helps with questioning
- requires execution of emotional control
- promotes self-control
- facilitates attention to key facts
- enhances memory
- organizes thoughts are they are coming in
- evaluates and orders information

You can invite your students to take notes during:
- A lecture
- A presentation
- A clip
- An audio story
- A visitor
- A tour
- Reading a book
- While working on a project

Creating Independence in your classroom

"Whether you think you can, or you think you can't--you're right."
— Henry Ford

- Start with the learning space design
- Keep materials visible and organized
- Set classroom jobs
- Create visuals for classroom routines
- Show classroom expectations
- Teach your students self-assessment when appropriate
- Teach your students self-reflection
- Teach your students metacognition

During your instruction, you can also follow this model by Dave and Jon Ferguson (2019)

- "I do, you **WATCH**"
- "I do, you **HELP**"
- "You **DO**, I help"
- "You **DO**, I watch"

Thinking Out Loud

"The most courageous act is still to think for yourself. Aloud."
- Coco Chanel

Thinking aloud gives the students the time and space to say what they are thinking while solving a problem, reading, or doing a project. Students become aware of their thinking process, the particular way they solve a problem, or even how they like or prefer learning!

Before you ask your students to think aloud, you need to model this to your students. For example, if you are teaching long division, it can go like this: "Three-hundred fifty-two divided by two. Hmmm. What do I do first? Oh, I know! I ask myself how many times two can go inside the three. One! Where do I put the one? I write it on top of the three. Then, I multiply one times two. One times two is two. I put this two under the three. Next, I subtract three minus two. Three minus two is one. After this, I bring down the five and write it by the one. Now, I have fifteen. It is time to start the same process all over again! How many times does the two go inside fifteen? Seven…"

It is all about verbalizing our inner speech or silent dialogue so our students know how to think their way through a problem. You can use this opportunity to make a common mistake on purpose and talk out loud while starting again trying to find a solution. This way, students go to the math problem or any other project with the peace of mind that mistakes are OK and that they are a part of learning. Not only that, they heard the kinds of words that you used when you made a mistake or encountered a roadblock. Modeling for students is not only important for hearing the process out loud but also to hear the mindset needed to work on things that can go wrong the first or second time!

Then, you can model how to reflect on a finished or unfinished project by saying and encouraging your students to say the following things:

- So far, I've learned...
- This made me think of...
- That didn't make sense.
- I think ___ will happen next.
- I reread that part because...
- I was confused by...
- I think the most important part was...
- That is interesting because...

- I wonder why...
- I just thought of…

By doing this, you are training and helping your students enjoy and celebrate the process of learning, not just the final and "right" answer!

Self-explaining

"If you can't explain it simply, you don't understand it well enough."
- Albert Einstein

Self-explaining is a cognitive practice that helps learners be aware of their learning process, notice where they are stuck, and celebrate their understanding. "Self-explanation involves students trying to explain concepts to themselves in their heads" (Sumeracki, 2020). This strategy comes after you have taught them how to think out loud. After students master the skill of thinking out loud to solve problems or work on projects, they can start the self-explanation out loud or in their minds.

When you teach or use this and all the other strategies with your students, remember to share the **why** of these strategies. They will appreciate why you are using them. They will also start using them on their own before you know it because they have noticed how effective they are!

Self-explanation:
- helps them be aware of their learning experience
- shows them where they are stuck
- helps them to realize how much they know and what link they are missing to understand everything
- helps them organize and store that information in a way that makes sense to them

- empowers them since they are totally active in their learning
- helps them celebrate their learning.

Metacognition

"To make an individual metacognitively aware is to ensure that the individual has learned how to learn." - Garner

Metacognition is thinking about your thinking and learning process. It is trying to understand how you learn and remember things better. It is reflecting on your way of thinking and your learning experience. Metacognition means "thinking about thinking" (Oakley and Shewe, 2021, pgs. 114 & 115).

As teachers, we are constantly reflecting on our practices, and on how we can help our students use higher-order thinking strategies so they can better learn and remember concepts and skills. We are always thinking about how students think! You are reading this book because you are reflective of your teaching practices. You love improving intellectually and professionally. We even have journals or leave a place in our lesson plans to reflect on how a lesson or unit went. Now, "Do we encourage our students to be reflective? Do we provide them with opportunities to analyze their learning?" (Joseph, 2003). Let's model this to our students out loud and give them the time and space to exercise metacognition! Start small. This is not an easy and simple skill that can be learned the first time. Have them practice this frequently until it becomes a habit!

Questions you can model for your students so they can use them later while doing their assignments

- Have I solved a problem like this before?
- What did I do that worked before?

- Do I feel like I understand this?
- Or am I stuck?
- What else should I try?
- Whom can I ask for help?
- Did I get it right?
- What did I do that was different from last time?
- How can I do better?
- Did I find a strategy that can help me again?
- Will I be able to do this again?
- Should I write the steps I used to solve this problem?
- How does this make me feel?
- Can I explain what I just learned to my classmates or parents?
- I wonder if there is an easier way to solve this?
- How can I remember this on the test?
- Was this too easy or too hard for me?

Students can also verbalize their metacognition while solving a math problem, writing a paragraph, answering questions to a social studies question, and working on a project.

Brain Teasers

"Take rest; a field that has rested gives a bountiful crop." - Ovid.

Brain teasers give the brain a break from working or focusing hard! Brain teasers or breaks come in many forms and sizes. I prefer brain breaks that involve movement. I think the best brain break is to go out and take a walk or free play for a few minutes, like a short recess! But, if you can't afford that between each class period, you can be creative and make it work for your students.

Benefits of using brain teasers with your students:

- Break from highly focused activities
- Reduce cognitive load
- Alert the brain again
- Calm the brain depending on the brain break
- Can attend to students' social and emotional needs
- Improve memory
- Increase time on task
- Boost attention and motivation
- Help students think creatively and critically
- Reduce boredom
- Make students laugh
- Reduce stress, burnout, and anxiety
- Take a break from cognitive load
- Decreasing cognitive load

Brain teasers can be done at the beginning of each class, in between classes, and at the end of the school day! These are some examples of brain teasers you can do in your classroom:

- Board games
- Brief walk outside or inside the classroom
- Charades
- Coloring
- Crosswords
- Dance to action songs
- Deep breathing
- Do nothing for a minute
- Drawing or writing in a journal
- Hands-on projects
- Have your students jump
- Heads Up, Seven-Up!
- Icebreakers

- Jokes
- Lateral thinking problems
- Let them daydream
- Make different facial gestures
- Minute to win it
- Movement
- Optical illusions
- Painting
- Pattern problems
- Play calming music
- Puzzles
- Riddles
- Simon Says
- Sing silly song
- Spot the difference
- Stretch
- Sudoku
- Take imaginary trips
- Tell a story
- Tic, Tac, Toe
- Tongue Twisters
- Use a sensory bin
- Word search

Journaling

"A journal is your completely unaltered voice." — Lucy Dacus

Have you ever felt relaxed and light after journaling? That is because journaling reduces stress, anxiety, and overthinking! It helps you get your thoughts out of your head and down on paper. Journaling is not only great for adults but for students too, even if they doodle instead of writing words. "Journaling helps students be less restrained when expressing themselves. It also gives students time to organize their thoughts" (Schweighofer, 2022).

You can use students' journals to learn more about your students and use them as an assessment tool. When you take a few moments to read your students' academic journals, you can see how they think and learn. You can read their minds! You can have two types of journaling practices in your classroom. Students can have a personal and an academic journal!

Questions to help your students' journal:
- "What did you learn today?"
- "How does this connect or relate to what we already know?"
- "How can this help you today and/or in the future?"
- "How did this make you feel?"

Tips for making journaling fun:
- Provide a notebook and special pens or pencils just for that
- Your students can do it at the end of some subjects
- Your students can do it at the end of the day
- Your students can do it once a week (like my students!)

These are some types of journals that you or your students can use:
- writing journal
- bullet journal
- dream journal
- art journal
- doodle journal
- prayer journal
- reading journal
- gratitude journal
- workout journal
- mental journal
- idea journal

- goal journal
- mood journal
- reflective journal
- academic journal

Loops and review

"Repetition creates the master." - Cesar Millan

Loop is the art of bringing it home! I love listening to podcasts, especially when the host reminds me at the end of the conversation about all the points she mentioned throughout the episode! I finish listening with a sense of clarity and am ready for action or reflection. The information settles in my brain in an organized way, therefore I understand it better! I am sure that happens to you too! I wonder if our students can have the same reaction after we have a mini-lesson or lecture! If not, bring it home!

By "looping" or reviewing at the end of a lesson or unit, you help your students make sense of what they just learned and the loss of learning will be less over time. This is how you can do it:

- After a unit, review quickly each lesson.
- Do the same at the end of the quarter for all the units!
- Do the same at the end of the year. Go over the highlights of each unit!
- Use games, art, storytelling, and graphic organizers to bring a sense of closure to your lesson or unit.
- Do this when you give a lot of information when you talk to friends, colleagues, students, friends, etc.!
- Celebrate the end of the unit by reminding your students how hard they worked on certain concepts and skills.
- You can ask questions about what they learned.
- Bring it home!

Curse of knowledge

"The only true wisdom is in knowing you know nothing." Socrates

Ouch! This sounds harsh! You and I might have this type of curse! We teachers can be in danger of forgetting that our students don't have all the background knowledge we do as we explain new and old concepts to them. This is called "cognitive bias," and it is something that can be innocently done. That is why we need to be intentional when we explain new concepts or skills or even review them! We need to try to explain things, supposing that they don't have any background knowledge on the matter. That way we can start from the very basics!

"The curse of knowledge is the phenomenon of thinking something is easy or obvious because you have had a lot of experience with it" (Nickerson, 1999). "Though we, of course, were also once students who did not know anything about the subject we are teaching, it is hard for us to "unlearn" the information and put ourselves in a student's shoes to experience the novelty of learning about this concept" (Weinstein, Sumeracki, Caviglioli, 2019, pg. 47).

Since it is impossible for us to get into our students' heads to see exactly what they know or what they don't, we can use the following strategies:

- Assess for previous knowledge
- Use analogies and metaphors
- Show clips
- Ask what they know about that concept or skill before presenting it
- Use familiar scenarios
- Listen to your students/children
- Visit their world
- Use of clips

- Context
- Real-time feedback
- Connections
- Break concepts and skills into small chunks
- Break-in between to reflect

The term and idea behind the phrase "curse of knowledge" was coined in a 1989 Journal of Political Economy article by economists Colin Camerer, George Loewenstein, and Martin Weber. Now, this phrase is applied to many fields!

Avoid digital busywork

"Kids don't remember their best day of television." Author Unknown

Just as there is such a thing as "busy worksheets," we can fall into providing digital activities that do not lead to true learning. We know that there are so many apps that we can have our students use, but sometimes it is just difficult to differentiate what digital resources are going to help with learning from the ones that are just "fun!" Going through the decision of what is best for our students can be overwhelming because there are so many digital resources for our students in this era! They are all fun, engaging, and stimulating.

So, make sure you decide wisely and don't go with digital resources or apps that
- just look fun
- just look cute
- just have low-level comprehension questions or activities

Make sure you use the few that provide meaningful and lasting learning experiences. Have your students use technology to create meaningful learning experiences that include inquiry, problem-solving, and higher-order thinking skills. If you can provide meaningful learning experiences without the use of technology or screen time, go ahead and have your students use what they have in the classroom or at home! Hands-on is always better. I know that apps, screen time, and technology are fun, bright, and entertaining. But, ask yourself every time they are in front of a screen: Are my students creating content? Solving problems? Or, are they just consuming content? Just doing busy work that looks like a lower-thinking skill that would be even boring on paper?

Remember that our students will need a break from screen time. Doodling, journaling, collages, use of natural objects, and so many other things can be used to show understanding and mastering of concepts and skills! Let's focus first on the priorities you have for our students and then, let's look for the best tools to do that to the best of our ability!

Have them use a real pencil!

"A #2 pencil and a dream can take you anywhere". - Joyce Meyer

Using a pencil (or pen, crayon, color pencil, marker!) involves more senses and motor skills than using a screen.
When students use a pencil, they have the following pros:

- Relaxation
- Creativity
- Handwriting forces your brain to mentally engage with the information, improving both literacy and reading comprehension.
- Flow
- Engages the brain

- Focusing the brain
- Calming the brain
- Spatial memory
- Hand-eye coordination
- Opportunities to doodle
- Use of fine-motor skills

Let's have our students use more pencils, even during online learning! Remember that not for every single assignment, students need to write with pencils. If the writing can be done with different writing tools, go for it! Such as drawing on sand, finger painting, markers, brushes, letter collages from magazines, plastic letters, magnet letters, and objects that can make up letters. The options are infinite!

Worksheets

"I write to discover what I know." -Flannery O'Connor

I am not against using worksheets in the classroom, nor in favor of using them all the time. Using worksheets is like everything else; we can't always do the same thing. But using worksheets is not a bad strategy if they target higher-order thinking skills! It is the same with colorful apps; if they don't target higher-order thinking skills and students don't create with the information given, or don't have a meaningful learning experience, the tool is not powerful. Like everything else, worksheets are a tool. You can use them as you wish, so no worries or don't feel bad if you use worksheets. You need to do what you know is best for your students and **you do**!

Drilling

"If people knew how hard I had to work to gain my mastery, it would not seem so wonderful at all." — Michelangelo Buonarroti

Drilling is not a bad thing! Drilling when done in a fun and consistent way is powerful and extremely necessary. Drilling brings mastery, confidence, familiarity, and fluency. Students need to master some concepts really well before they can apply them to real-life scenarios or move to more complex and multi-step problems.

You can drill multiplication facts, addition, subtraction, division facts, states and capitals, sight words, grammar rules, map skills, and so many things that you know are necessary to tackle harder concepts! This is a powerful tool that doesn't sound fun, but it is effective! Speaking about fun, you can make it fun by adding music, movement, rituals, and gamification to your drilling routine!

Ask "ungoogleable" questions

"The wise man doesn't give the right answers, he poses the right questions."
- Claude Levi-Strauss

If the answer to the question you ask your students can be found online, students don't have to really think. That is why we need to ask questions that are open-ended but require a strong familiarity with the content. "Open-ended questions are an effective way to challenge your students and learn more about how they think. They encourage extended responses and allow your students to reason, think, and reflect" (Neely, 2019).

These are some questions you can ask your students:
- What is another way to do this?
- How did you come up with that answer?
- Why do you think the character did that?
- Can you demonstrate that?
- Can you formulate more questions for your classmates?
- How would you apply what you just read to solve this problem?
- Can you use this process to solve another type of problem?
- What did you understand from this lecture, clip, or chapter?
- What is the main idea?
- Can you compare and contrast these three concepts?
- What is the problem and solution in this chapter?
- What is the cause and effect in this chapter?
- What is the theme of this book?
- What is the purpose of this article?
- How does this apply to your life?
- Tell me in which ways you agree and disagree with this article.
- Can you give me an example based on this chapter?
- How does this make you feel?

Cognitive risk vs. cognitive load

"Tired, but mentally."- Shiquille Williams

"Cognitive load" relates to the amount of information that working memory can hold at one time. Our students' working memory has a limited capacity. This is why we need to avoid overloading our students' minds with busy work, extra instructions, and longer lectures, you get the point.

Everything that your students do takes up mental energy and it has a cognitive load. The more they think or stay on task, the more cognitive load they carry in their minds. Have the following in mind at the time of teaching in order to avoid cognitive overload:

- Provide movement and breaks during lessons
- Give clear and short directions
- Give directions one at a time
- For large projects, work in chunks
- Use dual coding (words and pictures) to give directions
- Avoid multi-tasking

Inversely, cognitive risk is:

- challenging our students to go deeper
- thinking critically
- solving problems
- applying concepts to real-life experiences
- instilling the love for the process of thinking and learning
- engaging in meaningful learning experiences
- giving time to process information
- not only **energizing** the brain but also giving time to **focusing** and **calming** your students' brains

Flow

"Surrender to the flow." - Mike Gordon

Have you ever been super focused and fully immersed in what you were doing? If so, you were in a state of flow! This is the optimal state for learning! This sounds easy but it is not. If you are like me, you barely have five minutes to yourself! That is why I wake up earlier than my family when I have focus-required things to do. Otherwise, all the distractions get in the way! I can see the difference in the quality of the final product when I am able to focus.

It is not easy to provide the time and space for students to reach a state of flow. Yet, we need to try our best to help our students experience this when they need to do something cognitively challenging because this is the ideal state for meaningful and lasting learning!

Ideas to facilitate flow in your classroom:

- Get your students to a "place where they fall so in love with learning that little else matters" (Wheeler, 2022).
- Provide the time and space for your students to do certain assignments silently or focused.
- Don't extend this time for too long. Sustained attention doesn't last forever!
- Make sure the level of challenge is in the right spot. The assignment for your students can't be too easy or too difficult. If it is too difficult, it will create anxiety. If it is too easy, it will create boredom.
- Try to do these types of high-focus required activities in their prime time, not at the end of the day.
- Clear distractions. Once, I put calm music on when my students were in focus mode and one student asked me, very kindly, to stop it because she couldn't concentrate. She was aware of her state of flow!
- We can ask students how we can help them achieve this state of flow.
- Work with your students' stamina and increment it little by little. You can show a chart by showing the minutes they can stay on task reading, writing, solving a problem, etc.
- Help them set goals to achieve during that state of flow.
- Right after they finish the task done in a state of flow, provide mental and physical breaks.
- Provide choice. We can't force a state of flow on students.

- They need to see a kind of reward for being in a state of flow, like an "accomplished task."
- Provide positive and immediate feedback at the end of the task.
- Most importantly, explain to your students the importance of being in a state of flow for certain things and give ideas of how that can be achieved in school and at home!

Chunking

"A miracle is when the whole is greater than the sum of its parts. A miracle is when one plus one equals a thousand." — *Frederick Buechner*

Having to read, understand, and study big concepts or chapters is very intimidating even for adults. Imagine what our students feel when they see this enormous mountain of things to do, memorize, or learn. We need to assure them that we will cross that mountain, but we will do it a few steps at a time! This is called "chunking," a process that helps us absorb large pieces of information by doing it little by little or in chunks. There are two ways to chunk:

One is when students control how they are going to memorize, for example, all the countries in Africa. They start with two or three. The next day, they memorize a few others while saying the previous ones as well, and so on. They do this until they learn and memorize all the countries! Provide opportunities for your students to learn how to chunk while memorizing. In the beginning, you can chunk information for them until they can do it for themselves!

The other way to chunk is done by the teacher. When you teach your students how to read, you teach in chunks that build on each other. You do this slowly and follow your students' pace. You students need to dwell on each part of the process before they can move on!

Sleep

> *"Sleep does more than simply give students the energy they need to study and perform well on tests. Sleep actually helps students learn, memorize, retain, recall, and use their new knowledge to come up with creative and innovative solutions."*
> *- Kelly Cappello*

This is the only strategy that you can't put into practice in your classroom, but you can still talk about its importance with your students while inspiring them to go to bed early! I am sure you have suffered before from sleep deprivation. Your focus and attention the next day are not the same. When this happens to students, they can't learn efficiently. "Sleep itself has a role in the *consolidation of memory*, which is essential for learning new information" (Ellenbogen, Payne, and Stickgold, from the Division of Sleep Medicine at Harvard Medical School).

Sleep plays a huge role in memory and learning. But first, let me tell you what the science of learning has found about the process or cycle of learning:

- **Encoding or acquisition:** introduction of new information to the brain.
- **Consolidation or storage:** the brain makes sense of this information and stores it.
- **Recall or retrieval:** is getting that information out of the brain.

"Acquisition and recall occur only during wakefulness, but research suggests that **memory consolidation takes place during sleep** through the strengthening of the neural connections that form our memories" (Ellenbogen, Payne, and Stickgold).

Wow! Students need to have a good night of sleep to be able to **consolidate** information, concepts, and knowledge in their long-term memory. So, remind them about the importance and relationship between memory, learning, and sleep and give them ideas for a good night of sleep. These are some ideas to sleep better:

- read a book before bed
- go to bed early
- be consistent on the time they go to bed
- eat a few hours before sleeping
- avoid screen time right before going to bed
- avoid stimulating drinks and food
- take deep breaths before going to bed
- journal before going to bed
- exercise during the day
- think happy thoughts before going to sleep

1 mind + 1 mind= 3 minds

"No two minds ever come together without, thereby, creating a third, invisible, intangible force which may be likened to a third mind." — Napoleon Hill

One of the dynamics that we cannot afford to lose in the classroom is **collaboration** among our students, whether they are together in the classroom or miles away while connecting virtually! Give your students the time and space for collaboration because when **two** minds get together, **three** are at work!!! I am paraphrasing what Napoleon Hill wrote in 1939!

Who doesn't want this! Besides the third mind, students can bond, grow, and bloom when they work in smaller groups! We know this, we just have to try to use this modality more often. We can start little by little. You and your students will love the results!

The Rule of 3

"It is what we know already that often prevents us from learning."
- Claude Bernard.

There is a reason behind these three-letter brands: BBC, NBA, GAP, UPS, TPT, MTV, CAT, IBM, and so many more.

Phrases:
- "Life, liberty, and the pursuit of happiness"
- "Government of the people, by the people, for the people"
- "Blood, sweat, and tears"
- "Stop, drop, and roll"
- "Location, location, location"
- "Mind, Body & Spirit"
- "Life, liberty, and the pursuit of happiness"
- "Government of the people, by the people, for the people"
- "Liberté, Égalité, Fraternité" (French motto)

Stories:
- Three Blind Mice
- Three Little Pigs
- Three Musketeers
- "Goldilocks and the Three Bears"
- The Three Wise Men

"The "rule of three" is based on the principle that things that come in threes are inherently funnier, more satisfying, or more effective than any other number" (GigaSavvy, 2014). So, when you teach, try to present three concepts or directions at the most. Create a phrase or letters that go along with those concepts so students can make more sense of it and remember it more easily!

Learning and applying knowledge from other fields

"Learning from other people is what music is all about." - Neil Young

As you may have noticed already, I am applying concepts from other fields other than pedagogical strategies to use with our students. This is a great strategy to keep your teaching strategies fresh. There are so many things that work in nature, business, psychology, gamification, and neuroscience that we can apply in our classrooms! Those are principles and principles can be adapted to best fit our students' needs! In sum, don't consume *just* teacher content!

- read books from other fields
- listen to podcasts from other fields
- find hobbies and share them with your students
- follow people and hashtags that are not about teaching
- be interested in other people's interests
- engage in conversations other than teacher-related topics
- go on a trip and learn something new about another culture
- listen to another radio
- teaching is just a part of you, not the *whole* you!

This will refresh your ideas, will help you innovate, take a break, and have a bigger picture at the time of teaching a lesson or new unit.

After all, "great innovators apply ideas from fields other than their own," says Carmine Gallo says in his book Talk Like Ted (2014). What other passions do you have that might have disappeared from your life? Are you ready to bring them back?! Mine are: playing piano as I used to (that would be nice!), learning French, exercising more, feeding my spirit, traveling, traveling, and traveling!

Hexagonal Thinking

"If everyone is thinking alike, then somebody isn't thinking." - George S. Patton

Hexagonal Thinking is an amazing strategy that allows you to see how your students think and how they associate with ideas, concepts, or words! First off, cut out small hexagons and write words or concepts on them. Each student receives the same set of hexagons with the same words on them. As you talk, teach a lesson, show a clip, etc. students connect those hexagons in a way it makes sense to them! Then, they glue them on a poster and see their thinking displayed! I love having my students see what their classmates did with their hexagons. We can see our different way of thinking and connecting ideas!

"Hexagonal Thinking has been prevalent in the business world for some time now. It is, however, relatively new in the world of education. Hexagonal thinking is a method for considering connections between topics, ideas, and subject areas. It can even be done in grades as low as Kindergarten with pictures!" (Nelson-Danley, 2021)

It is amazing because students can associate, expand, find new correlations, and think critically. Teachers can use Hexagonal Thinking for meaningful cross-curricular integration and as a formative assessment. Hexagonal thinking can help students link concepts and ideas, and make connections between various subject areas.

This is creative and deep thinking! And these are the benefits:

- discussion
- creative thinking
- collaboration
- reflection
- deep discussion
- connections and associations

- deep thinking
- students realize that they think differently than their classmates
- it is so fun and interesting to compare the end product with others

How?
- In a hexagonal thinking exercise, students are given hexagonal tiles with ideas, questions, or facts which they arrange, so that related tiles are next to each other.
- With higher levels of understanding, students can explain the relationships between sets of tiles.
- Hexagonal thinking can also be used to help plan a project or map out the problem-solving process.
- Students can fill in their blank hexagons and arrange them to demonstrate their ideas.

Receiving and retrieving

"Education is what remains after one has forgotten what one has learned in school." - Albert Einstein

You and I know that in learning, *what comes in must come out!* We tend, though, to use instructional strategies that explain, digest, "put-inside," etc. This is all good, but we also need to make sure we use instructional strategies (retrieval practices) that allow students to:

- recall info, concepts, and skills without looking at their textbooks
- think-pair-share
- brain dump
- reflect on journals
- retrieve things from yesterday, last week, last month, and even last year!

Students will retrieve better when they practice this more often with you, themselves, and in groups!

Dual coding

"One picture is worth a thousand words." - Fred R. Barnard

Dual coding is when you use images and words at the same time to explain one concept, give directions, teach a skill, etc. When we use different types of stimuli, students are able to better encode and retrieve information. (Clark, 2021).

When we use images and text to explain a concept or idea, students encode, consolidate, and retrieve these things in their memory in a more effective way. You can provide the pictures and place them by concepts as you explain them. Or, your students can draw or find the pictures to place them by their vocabulary words, concepts, definitions, directions, and skills that they are learning from you or their textbook.

These are the things on which your students can use text and images:
- timeline
- infographics
- storyboards
- stories
- comics & cartoons
- note-taking
- social media posts
- posters
- diagrams
- doodling
- maps
- flashcards

Anticipate errors

"An ounce of prevention is worth a pound of cure." - Benjamin Franklin

I still remember when my professor told me we had to start using an updated version of APA. She mentioned the exact changes and that saved me a lot of time researching everywhere! That is when I started seeing a difference between two kinds of mistakes and how to approach them as a teacher!

We want students to **make** mistakes. We want them to learn from them. The cognitive process that goes behind allowing students to make mistakes and learning from them is amazing **and** needed! There are some other errors that we **can** anticipate before they go to work on their assignments!

We can say, for example:

- "Remember that we indent at the beginning of each paragraph. We tend to do it in the first paragraph and forget to do it at the beginning of the second one!"
- "Remember to add the 0 on the second line when you do multiplication. This is a common mistake!"
- "Remember we need to pause when we encounter periods."
- "Remember that the number 0 has the same height as the other numbers!"
- "Remember to finish with a question mark if you are asking a question."

In sum, there are technical mistakes that we can help students avoid. The mistakes that help students learn right from wrong, or the mistakes that help them refine a product, are OK to make, and we need to let them make them!

Concept attainment

"Even the genius asks questions." –Tupac Shakur

Concept Attainment is a constructivist approach to teaching and learning drawn from the work of Jerome Bruner (1956). In this instructional model, students apply their prior understanding to determine the attributes of a concept through the processes of comparing and contrasting. This structured inquiry approach gives students the opportunity to:

- distinguish between relevant and irrelevant information
- observe, classify, and hypothesize
- connect newly attained concepts with old information
- think inductively

You can show examples of things that are not what the concept is about or what it doesn't mean, basically "non-examples." Then, you show what that word means. You go back and forth showing what it is and what is not. You can also ask your students to tell you about each picture or phrase. That way, the concept is being attained!!!

More about concept attainment
- It is all about clarifying concepts and ideas!
- You don't say the definition of the word, idea, concept, etc... right away.
- You present examples and "not" examples.
- Students guess the concept by figuring out the common attributes. You must choose concepts or ideas that have clear characteristics.
- This can be done with words, pictures, characteristics, attributes, etc.
- Remember to have two columns, so students don't mix up the examples with the "not" examples!

Reciprocal Teaching

"The art of teaching is the art of assisting discovery." - Mark Van Doren

Your students will love this strategy and you will work less! They will also remember what they have learned using this strategy! Divide your class into groups of four or any number you see best for your number of students, using break-out rooms or in your classroom by just forming groups!

After you form groups among your students, you can assign roles to each student in that group. These are the roles/tasks that Vygotsky's theory proposes:

- Summarizer: one student is in charge of summarizing what the group reads.
- Questioner: after the group reads the chapter or paragraphs, one student lists all the possible questions based on that reading.
- Clarifier: one student is in charge of clarifying or answering questions.
- Predictor: one student predicts what the answer might be.

You can have fewer or more roles to fit your students' needs or simply to work with your preferences. Students can take turns in these roles as they read the entire chapter or article. While students do this, the teacher makes sure each student delivers the role properly. As the students become more confident in each role, the teacher can let them work more independently.

You can bet that at the end of the chapter or article, students really understand what they just read! It is a very interactive way of making students comprehend what they are reading! Don't you think?

Uncluttered worksheets

"But first, declutter." — Julie Hage

Students get distracted when their worksheets are busy, even with cute images on them. Students need to focus on the task, and having an uncluttered worksheet is better for their minds! The following are things to consider at the time of choosing a worksheet (PPP, Google doc, or slide) for your students:

- less is more
- no unnecessary images
- clear fonts
- dual coding, directions can be accompanied by an image that helps your students understand them better
- not too many colors
- clear margins
- more space than images or words
- important information can be in bold or underlined
- easy eye path to get from point A to B (not things all over the place)
- make sure that there is only the necessary information on worksheets, so students can **focus** on what is **important**

Cute is not the primary goal. Meeting our students' brain needs is!

Uncluttered curriculum

Ask yourself these questions and reflect on your answers:
- Do you keep old textbooks, worksheets, workbooks, practice sheets, etc.? Why?
- Do you have a system that works for you?

- Does that system need to improve?
- On which standard do you base your decision about keeping or throwing/donating items, textbooks, resources, objects, etc.?
- Do you just keep just what you need curriculum-wise?
- Are you intentional about having in your classroom just what you need for your students' optimum and effective learning experience?

Uncluttered mind

"If you take care of your mind, you take care of the world."
- Arianna Huffington

How do we do this when we receive about 11 million pieces of information per second from our nerve ends? I think teachers receive even more!!!

This is how we can have uncluttered minds, or at least have less to have more focus and clarity!

- declutter your physical space
- avoid multitasking
- limit the amount of information you consume: digital and physical media
- write your thoughts
- meditate and/or pray
- limit your social media consumption
- unfollow, so you don't have to keep up with thousands of people's lives
- watch less screen
- unplug
- walk without listening to anything

- spend time in silence
- go to bed early without looking at a screen
- walk in nature
- detox from digital input
- take deep breaths
- leave your phone in another room
- delete apps
- put your phone in silence
- leave most of your notifications off
- read books
- say "no" more often
- let go
- clean your computer's desktop
- unsubscribe
- **less is more** for your mind!

How do **you** declutter your mind?!

Brain dumps

"The greatest freedom is to be free of our own mind." - *Osho*

There are certain things you teach that need to go to your students' long-term memory. And you know what those things are: information that is needed to solve problems, the knowledge that needs to be present before you teach something else, and so on. In order to help your students store information in their long-term memory, they need not only to get information "in," but also "out" of their brains! In the classroom, usually, students only receive information. They are not challenged enough to retrieve what we put inside their brains. One simple retrieval strategy (knowledge going out) is **brain dumps.**

This is how you can do it:

- Take a moment at the end or in the middle of a lesson, lecture, or slides to ask your students to get a paper and pencil.
- Ask your students to write everything they can remember.
- They can read that to you or their classmates.
- You can ask your students to write what they just learned, or something they remember from the last lesson, unit, etc.
- Do not use this activity for a grade. Tell your students before they do it that you will not grade this activity. Share with them the importance of this learning strategy. It is all about helping them, not a testing activity.

Spacing and Spiraling

"Repetition creates the master."- Cesar Millan

Have you been guilty of cramming information or reading lots of chapters the night before the test? I have! And I know many of my students did it at one point, only to find out that it didn't work so well! My major at my university was Piano. I played piano since I was very little too and since then; I learned that cramming practices were never a good idea. Even worse, it affected the quality of my performance. As my teachers always told me, "Yanina, practicing every single day for a few minutes is better than practicing piano for hours the day before our lesson." The same is true with remembering information. Skills and knowledge need to be practiced throughout a long period of time to be in our students' long-term memory. Spacing and spiraling do take time to do as a teacher and as a student, but these practices are so much more powerful than cramming.

Spacing is when you "space" similar concepts and skills, so you do not cram them all at once and move on to another unit. You return to the same content frequently so the information and skills can be consolidated and retrieved again and again!

Spiraling is when you "spiral" different concepts and skills frequently. It is more of a mix of concepts and skills. Please use both! If you do this and frequently, whatever you teach, will go to long-term memory!

Audience

"To have great poets, there must be great audiences." - Walt Whitman

Provide a real audience for your students' writing, science projects, social studies projects, and math projects! Do this and your students will take learning more seriously!!! Provide a real audience for their finished work! Why?

- Students who think of their audience while they work, take their assignment more seriously.
- Students discover their voice.
- They know they can cause an impact.
- An audience gives students an authentic and meaningful purpose that can guide them through the entire creation process.

Ways to bring "authentic" audience (I never force students to share in front of their classmates. Many times after a while, they tell me that they can do it!)
- Blogging
- Vlogging
- Authors' Night
- Living Wax Museum
- Bulletin board
- Peer sharing
- Sharing on a classroom stage
- Reading from their desks

- Writing for grants
- Design thinking
- Helping the community
- Solving a real problem
- Writing a song
- Writing for a newsletter or magazine
- Project-based learning
- Design Thinking

Talking about the relevance of the topic is great, but creating content for a "real" audience is different and you might see better quality work!

Storyboard

"By failing to prepare, you are preparing to fail." – Benjamin Franklin

A storyboard is where students put the ideas, illustrations, and sequence for their stories. It is a tool to plan a story. This helps students to do a lot of thinking and tweaking elements before they even begin writing the story. They get a chance to **interactively** plan their setting, main character, secondary characters, problem, solution, scenes, etc. before they put it into writing! They can use drawings, graphics, objects, video, anything… to plan the different elements of their story.

For a few years now, I have noticed how differently my students write when they plan their writing first. We spend a couple of days planning the theme, climax, paragraphs, intro, transitional phrases and so many things for that specific type of writing. For storyboards, we use doodles, 3D objects, drawings, scavenger hunts, games, templates, recipes, anything!

We also have a sensory experience before each writing unit. When we want to write in sequence, for example, we make slime or other things that require multiple steps. The next day, we write about that experience. My students remember the steps and use beautiful transitional phrases. They tend to write more because they had the experience where they can refer to while writing.

When we write narrative essays, we take a walk and write five things we see, hear, touch, smell, etc. When it is time to write, my students refer to those multi-sensory experiences. They use those memories or notes to add them to the story instead of telling me they do not know what to write because they ran out of ideas!

Remember to have a sensory experience before each writing unit and use a template to organize and collect ideas! The words will come naturally on their papers!!!

Time and space to think

"Our souls need time to think, dream, and reflect." - Jo Ann Davis

Students need to spend time thinking to perform certain focus-required tasks and enjoy learning. Even more, to enjoy the **process** of thinking and learning. If we don't provide our students with some time and space during school to think, they might not have that opportunity anywhere else.

This is how you can do it with your students:

- provide time and space for your students to **just** think
- you can give them five minutes after they have read/discussed/watched something to just think, before jumping to writing/talking about it
- you can provide five minutes before they start a

- test/assignment/etc. to just think
- just the *act of thinking* is crucial
- creativity, ideas, organization, metacognition, self-explanation clarity, and so many other *good* things happen when we provide students with the *time and space* to just think!
- students need five minutes (less or more, depending on your students) to reset and be ready for the next learning experience
- resting and thinking are not just a break from work, it is the requisite for better work

Interdisciplinary approach

"It is a narrow mind which cannot look at a subject from various points of view."
- George Eliot

Whenever you teach a concept, unit, or skill from two or more different approaches, you are teaching from an interdisciplinary approach! This approach is amazing because this is how we adults solve a problem in real-time in the real world. We use different areas to assess and solve a problem. We don't say, "Let me solve this problem using just my math skills." In reality, when we encounter a problem, we unconsciously use all the skills we have to solve it. We do not think "in subjects." We take an interdisciplinary approach to not only solve problems but to learn new things! We just do it this way because it is the natural thing to do. That is why we need to take this natural way of learning and apply it to our way of teaching!

By providing an interdisciplinary approach, students:
- gain better perspective
- analyze bias
- understand a concept from different perspectives
- get ready for the real world, which is now

- get a bigger picture of what they are learning

Nothing is solved/understood/appreciated by **just one** approach, right?!

Thematic Units

"You never really understand a person until you consider things from his point of view." - Harper Lee

Thematic units are similar to taking an interdisciplinary approach to teaching a topic or a standard. The difference with thematic units is that you can build a whole unit, including many standards, or topics!

Thematic units:
- Create meaningful, real-world contexts for standards-based teaching and learning.
- Save work in the long run.
- Provide deep learning, students can make connections to other things they learn.
- Bring standards to a different dimension.
- Facilitate a better learning experience by providing a larger context. Students begin to see relationships and connections across time, place, and disciplines.
- Allow you to teach content using wider themes related to concepts.
- Resemble how life is experienced outside of school.

Have this in mind when choosing a topic or a group of standards
- Standards that can be grouped
- Choose the main area
- Hard-to-tackle concepts can be used for this
- What resources are available

- Field trips
- Guest speakers
- Garage sales/Thrift shops
- Technology
- Volunteers

Planning the Unit
- Choose the main standard and then create a web around it.
- Add standards to the integrated subjects.
- There is *no* limit to your creativity!
- Be open to suggestions from your students, volunteers, or room mother.
- Send an email to your student's parents telling them about your plans. They get excited and there are always parents who want to help/donate things.

Instructional Conversations

"All problems exist in the absence of a good conversation." - Thomas Leonard

When students talk about what they are learning or thinking, they are holding "instructional conversations." Instructional conversations take place when the teacher gives students the time and space to express their takeaways, talk about their experiences related to the content, exchange ideas with classmates, talk reflectively, and elaborate on their thinking. This is a great strategy to be able to "see and hear" what students are thinking!

So, got a "talkative" class? Give your students time and space to talk about what they have just learned. This is a "retrieval" (going out of their brains) strategy, therefore it is *great* as a study skill! Let your students talk. If they talk, they learn! If you are the only one who does the talking, you might have a "quiet" class, but your students might not remember as much as if you let them talk! This doesn't mean that you need to allow your students to talk the whole school day. You know when it is best to use this strategy and when it is best to give them the time and space to focus while working silently.

When we allow our students to talk about what they are learning, to analyze, reflect, think critically, etc. we are getting knowledge "out" of their brains. Allowing students to have instructional conversations can be a great way to work on the imbalance we currently have, which is a lot of encoding and a little bit of retrieving. Instructional conversations will help your students, not only encode knowledge but also consolidate it and retrieve it as well!

More than Highlighting

"Learning is not the product of teaching. Learning is the product of the activity of learners." - John Holt

Highlighting is a great practice for studying or reviewing for a test, but make sure that you teach your students to do more than highlighting. The act of highlighting is about saving what we think is important to remember, but do we close the book after that and try to say the sentences we highlighted, or do we just close the book and leave the highlighted parts without repeating them? The complete and effective practice will be to try to say what we highlighted right after we did it, the next day, and the next, and the next, without looking at the book!

This is also what helps students remember and do better at tests. Model the following practices for your students so they know how to do it at home!

- spaced review
- brain dumps

- loops, frequent review
- have your students test themselves
- anything that helps students pull information **out** of their brains without looking at their textbooks.

Active recall

"Yesterday is but today's memory, and tomorrow is today's dream."
-Khalil Gibran

Active recall or also known as "The Testing Effect" is when we give students the time and space for self-assessment: not just re-reading the material. Not just highlighting. Not just reading and repeating. Instead, have them close their books and do brain dumps, test themselves, retest the next day, next week, and test their classmates.

When students retrieve information, they encounter the content again. Students need to encounter the content not just once or twice, but many times so they can have it available in their minds whenever they need it to build on it, solve problems, and apply it to their lives.

Check the facts!

"Rather than love, than money, than fame, give me truth."
- Henry David Thoreau

I know that this is not a strategy, but I didn't want to leave this important element out of this book. If you are like me, you love social media and scrolling to get new ideas for your students. You see amazing engaging lessons and it is hard not to think that we are not doing things right for our students.

Andrew Watson in his book *The Goldilocks Map* talks about branded teaching, he says that we need to repeatedly ask ourselves if we can trust the source, and if we trust the source, we still need to know if the research cited reasonably fits without or within our boundaries. "Does that research apply to *these* students learning *our* curriculum in *this* cultural context?" (2021, pg. 97). Watson says that when teachers, PD speakers, and even books talk about things as an exact recipe for teaching, this is called "branded teaching."

So, in order to avoid falling for it, we need to ask ourselves the following questions:

- How do you know that person is not making things up? That person will never do it on purpose, but maybe she is a bit biased.
- How do we know that a book/PD/speaker/conference/podcast/social media, everything we consume is valid and will help our students' learning process?

This is where you can start:

- Is that person citing an actual study?
- Is the study applicable to your subject, grade, population, community, etc.?
- Trendy does not mean that will help your students.
- For example, a study on rats said that they were stimulated with a lot of "decor" in the environment. There is a study that shows the opposite with people!!!
- When it comes to cognitive research, look for the ones done on people, in the same grade as your students... not animals!
- Start always your research on "Google Scholar."
- Research is not about "always" or "never."
- When presented with a new idea, "technology" resource, etc.,

don't be afraid to ask for evidence, studies, authors...
- Always put your students first.
- Cute is not our priority. In terms of learning, look for strategies that help your students bring what you teach to their long-term memory!
- Follow people who are researchers, citing studies. They might not have a lot of followers on their platform, but they know their stuff!!! We can learn from them to help our students.
- Be *aware* of branded teaching. Branded teaching is not based on research/studies.
- Put your students first!

Listening skills

"Most of the successful people I've known are the ones who do more listening than talking." --Bernard Baruch

Instead of saying, "Listen to me!" Help your students train their listening skills by using the **science and art** of listening!

Benefits of using podcasts, audios, or audio stories in your classroom:

- Exposition to rich vocabulary
- Exposition to mental imagery
- Listening comprehension leads to reading comprehension
- They help meet standards, especially "listening" standards
- Provide real-life and cross-curricula narratives
- Students improve attention
- With a transcript, audios build confidence and literacy
- They go perfectly with note-taking (which is the art of thinking!)
- You can use them to do "flipped classrooms" (assign listening to a podcast to discuss later in class)

- Students receive information in a fun and entertaining way

Infographics

"Infographics are used as a powerful tool to allow people to easily digest information through the use of visual data, charts, and statistics."
- Rosemary Williams

Infographics condense information using visual and text mediums. They are a great tool to "enhance learning and retention and accommodate cognitive learning" (Alford, 2019). You can use infographics in two ways: to use it to teach content and for your students to create content.

You can use infographics to teach new concepts, review old ones, and make learning more interactive and organized for your students. Every time I see infographics, I feel like I better understand the topic. The flow is clear and I see it from a better perspective.

When students use infographics, they feel free to go beyond using the traditional textbook or slide presentations. They can bring together images, data, design, story, flow, art, and many more things they feel close to in order to teach concepts to their classmates in a relevant way.

Infographics help students synthesize in a fun and meaningful way!
- Infographics are visual representations of information, data, or knowledge intended to present information quickly and clearly.
- They help students make sense of the content by researching, critiquing, and organizing it.
- Students feel in power by manipulating/rearranging the flow of information in a way it makes sense to them. When they do this, they review and retrieve information!

Infographics as a teaching strategy:
- Show an infographic to explain a complex concept.
- Infographics show the big picture.
- Infographics show a new concept in an organized way.
- You can introduce a new lesson/concept/skill to them.

Infographics to analyze information by students:
- Ask your students to analyze them.
- Ask students to discuss the infographic with their classmates.
- Ask students to go through the infographic self-explaining what they see by following the "flow" of it.

Infographics created by students
- Ask students to create an infographic of the lesson/concept/skill they just learned.
- Students can share their creations with their classmates.
- Students can use their created infographics to do peer-teaching or as a study skill.

Easy recall

"Nothing is ever really lost to us as long as we remember it."
- L.M. Montgomery

This type of recall cannot be simpler. You just pause the class, start the class or end the class with the following simple questions:

- What did you learn in math (or any other subject) yesterday?
- Do you remember what you learned last week?
- Do you remember what you learned last month?
- Do you remember what you learned last school year?
- Is there something that you wish to remember now?
- What can you do to remember what you learned yesterday?

- Next week, ask the same questions!

When you do this, you are training your students and their brains to retrieve information. They are used to only receiving information to retrieve it just before a test and only if a test is coming. In this way, whenever they are receiving knowledge, they know they will have to retrieve it often, and just the act of knowing that it will be retrieved students take this information in a more meaningful and lasting way!

Concept maps

"There are those who follow maps and those who make them." - Alberto Villoldo

Concept maps are visual representations of ideas, concepts, and information. You can use concept maps to teach and your students can use concept maps to organize information in the form of charts, tables, graphic organizers, diagrams, flowcharts, etc.! When students use concept maps, they master the content because they:

- Encode and Organize
- Clarify
- Synthesize
- Integrate and Associate
- Structure
- Retrieve
- Understand
- Connect new information, skills, and concepts.

To get ready-to-use concept maps and many graphic organizers, head over to my Brain-friendly Teacher Academy:

https://yanina-s-school.thinkific.com/courses/brainfriendlyteacherbookresources

Label it

"Those who know, do. Those that understand, teach." — Aristotle

Labeling plants, for example, is a common and great practice for students. But, don't stop there! You can also label:

- a paragraph
- an essay
- a word problem
- nature items

When you label a paragraph, for example, students will be more aware of its many parts and the parts will come clear when they read and write paragraphs on their own.

Makers

"It is in your hands to create a better world for all who live in it."
- Nelson Mandela

Hands-on learning allows students to make learning visible and tangible. Students can manipulate concepts that otherwise are abstract to their minds. They can experiment with a trial and error mindset, learn from their mistakes, and have fun trying new things by putting theory into practice. In doubt how to make learning meaningful? Go hands-on! Transform your students into makers!!!! This is why:

- stimulates cognition
- it doesn't overstimulate (like too much screen time does)
- creation is better than consumption
- relaxation

- creativity
- trial and error mindset
- problem-solving
- motor skills
- increases attention and retention
- sensory experiences
- decreases stress & anxiety
- there is nothing like active learning
- abstract concepts become visible
- abstract concepts can be manipulated
- freedom in seeking alternative solutions
- less sense of rush
- out-of-the-box thinking
- learning becomes real
- students are invited to look for solutions in the real world, which is now, not only in the future!

Origami

"Tearing the paper means you've stopped believing in the infinite possibilities of a square." — Tor Udall

I love seeing my students creating amazing things with paper! It is incredible the animals, flowers, and many other things that my students can do! I am so impressed with their abilities to follow directions and their fine motor skills!

"Origami, the ancient art of paper folding, has applications in the modern-day classroom for teaching geometry, thinking skills, fractions, problem-solving, and fun science" (Ramirez, 2015). Wow, did you get that? And there is even more!

Origami creations have the following benefits for your students:

- 3D perception
- spatial memory
- sequential thinking and skills
- eye-hand coordination
- math reasoning
- memory
- patience
- attention skills
- fractions
- geometry
- problem-solving
- attention to detail
- creativity

In Japan, teachers use origami to teach literature, math, and art. In my classroom, I use it to teach the part of a flower, habitats, landmarks, etc. My students love exploring concepts and skills using origami!

Embodied cognition

"The hand is the tool of tools." - Aristotle

Cognition is not the only thing that facilitates learning. Cognition needs the body-mind connection, as well. Sometimes we focus so much on studying the "learning process" from psychology, cognition, and abstract points of view that we forget that **"bodily action and perception** play a central role in cognitive development" (A study by Osgood-Campbell, 2015).

The mind needs the body!!!
Cognition needs sensory input for a true and lasting learning experience such as:

Practical Instructional Strategies to Create Lasting Learning

- manipulating objects
- moving around
- activities that require spatial skills
- activities that require spatial memory
- music
- touching different textures
- experience different flavors
- smelling different aromas
- using real maps
- using real objects
- cooking
- baking
- mixing
- building 3-D models
- using fine-motor skills
- using gross-motor skills
- making collages
- bringing math to life
- bringing a page from a book alive
- living museums and so many more ideas found in this book
- learning through Project-based learning
- learning through Design Thinking
- using a STEAM Lab
- using a Makerspace
- playing with wooden toys
- forming 3D objects with clay
- forming letters on a sandbox
- creating a storyboard with nature objects

For ready-to-use instructional strategies, go to:
https://yanina-s-school.thinkific.com/courses/brainfriendlyteacherbookresources

At the Brain-friendly Teacher Academy & Book Resources you will also find:

- instructional resources for a meaningful and lasting learning experience
- a master class taught by me
- templates for annual, unit, and daily lesson plans
- a simple and fun unit for your students to learn about their brain parts and functions, and *how they learn*!
- and many more resources to help you save time in your efforts to create **lasting learning**

Enjoy!!!
https://yanina-s-school.thinkific.com/courses/brainfriendlyteacherbookresources

Chapter 6: How do my Students Learn, Really?

So, how does learning happen? This is something that Educational Neuroscientists, Cognitive Psychologists, and researchers in the field of Science of Teaching and Learning love to study! Oh, and me too! Ohhh, and you too since you are holding this book!!!

I am a teacher, and my job is to make everything simple for my students. I also love to read lots of Educational Neuroscience books, listen to podcasts, watch videos, and translate them into practical tips for other teachers and me so we can easily apply them for meaningful and lasting learning. In this chapter, you will read in simple words how learning happens. This is how I like it too, we don't need big and fancy words to explain or understand hard concepts. We, teachers, always have a way to make things simple and practical. After all, we are in the business of explaining hard concepts in a way that is easy to digest! So, here it goes!

We have billions of neurons that connect to each other. This is called **synapses**. These neurons are involved in the absorption of sensory information that we get from the outside. This information is stored temporarily in short-term memory. Short-term memory receives all this information that we encounter in our daily lives.

Once information is processed in our students' short-term memory, their "brain's neural pathways carry these memories to the structural core, where they are compared with existing memories and stored in our long-term memory" (Ford, 2011). This is exactly what we need to do as teachers. We need to do everything we can for the important concepts, information, knowledge, and skills to be moved to our students' long-term memory. That way students can remember information in order to apply it in their real lives, and be stored for the next school year when the next teacher is going to use that background information to expand it to a new and more difficult level. They can simply have useful information available when they need it for conversations, associations, and problem-solving!

For learning to be stored in long-term memory and ready to be retrieved, we also need to associate new concepts with old ones. When two neurons interact, a strong connection is formed and therefore a stronger memory of that concept! But, when we don't connect new or more complex ideas to music, movement, novelty, humor, storytelling, group activities, games, emotions, art, etc. those neurons are isolated and quickly fade from our memory. I know you do this in your classroom. Whenever you teach something new, you connect it to old information. You associate standards with other books, fields, lessons, and conversations. When we do that, students can remember better and for longer periods of time!

Another way to bring information to long-term memory is to frequently revisit what we learn using retrieval practices, and all the practices mentioned in the previous chapter! This process also produces mastery and fluency. I am sure the word "fluency" is ringing so many bells in your head right now! We love when our students are fluent in math, reading, etc. That is why we provide fluency passages and exercises! There is not a fancy strategy or secret formula to help your students remember and help them store information in their long-term memory. But, there are simple and effective practices, such as retrieval strategies, that are effective because they are based on how your students' brains learn naturally.

But, do we know how our students' brains learn naturally? **Yes!** Let's take a look at just a few parts of our brains and how they relate to learning. This is not a brain anatomy book. So, for your and my sake, the explanations will be short, sweet, and practical - which is the point of this book!

Brain parts and functions related to the science of learning

We, teachers, are really busy and need simple, practical, and effective strategies to apply right away in our classroom so our students can enjoy a meaningful and lasting learning experience.

Frontal lobes

Your frontal lobes are directly located behind your forehead. They are the biggest lobes in your brain. They are in charge of making decisions, your personality, and all your executive functions. They are kind of a big deal! To meet your students' frontal lobe needs in your classroom, provide the space and time for students to show their personalities and make decisions!

To appreciate and show their personalities, you can take an **interest inventory** at the beginning of the school year. In this interest inventory, you can ask for their favorite color, music, game, pizza, movie, book, hobby, and even learning-related questions. Questions like their favorite subject, favorite way to learn for a test, and favorite activity in the classroom. I even ask them what their least favorite subject or thing to do at school is. The answers reveal a lot and give you ideas at the time of planning your lessons. It doesn't mean that you have to do only the favorite things for each student. We know that this is not always possible, but to start planning with this point of reference is a much better way to reach your students. Just the fact of asking for their favorite things, sends them a message that you care! Bonus points if you send all those questions answered by you on the other side of the questionnaire! It is a great way to see if you have things in common and get to know you a little better as a person and not just as another teacher!

The other element is to allow students to make decisions in your classroom. This is totally up to you, your class, the subject you teach, etc. There is always room to involve your students in the decision-making. These are some things on which your students can vote or make decisions:

- the theme of the next end-of-year/unit celebration
- evidence for formative or summative assessments
- plant or pet to get for the classroom
- the system they can have for their binders on their desks
- bank of ideas after finishing their assignments
- class prizes
- field trips
- project-based learning ideas
- review games
- mnemonics to remember information
- ask them about things they would like to choose in class!

After you have started small, you can move on to bigger decisions according to the age of your group and dynamics!

Prefrontal Cortex

The prefrontal cortex is part of the frontal lobes, "located at the forward-most part of the skull. It's responsible for complex, high-functioning behaviors, like planning, decision-making, and personality expression" (Guy-Evans, 2021).

Here are a few ways to promote executive functioning in your students and develop their prefrontal cortices to improve attention span, listening skills, and other classroom-friendly traits recommended by Matthew Lynch (2019) in his article "How to train students to use their prefrontal cortex to pay better attention."

- promote active listening
- take time to review before teaching something new
- set a clear classroom routine

He says that "Creating an environment with the right balance of **structure and exploration** is key to promoting prefrontal cortex development."

Parietal Lobes

The parietal lobes are in charge of receiving and processing sensory information from the outside world through touch, taste, and temperature.

Below is a list of some of the associated functions of the parietal lobes:
- sensory information processing (e.g. touch, pain, pressure, and temperature).
- spatial mapping and attention
- visuospatial processing

- coordination of movement
- reading
- writing number representation (mathematics)

Occipital Lobes

The occipital lobes take care of visual perceptions, including color, form, orientation, visual data, and motion.

Below is a list of some of the associated functions of the occipital lobes:
- assessing size, depth, and distance
- determining color information
- object recognition
- face recognition
- mapping the visual world

When we go to a museum, an amusement park, a zoo, etc. we receive a map and usually, the people working there have name tags. This is done for an important reason: to avoid visitors getting lost. If you are like me, you are still confused about that place and how to get from point A to point B. I am sure when our students come to a new school, a new classroom, they feel the same.

It will be super helpful to provide our students with:

- a map of the classroom showing labeled things and their functions
- a name tag for every student showing how to pronounce names
- a dual-coding schedule, showing text and pictures
- how to get to important places from their classroom
- a diagram showing what to expect in the organization of their

desks
- diagrams, flow charts, anchor charts, infographics
- helpful images everywhere!

Cerebral Cortex

The cerebral cortex is the outer surface of the brain, and it is in charge of:
- higher-level processes such as conscious thought, emotion, reasoning, language, and memory.
- **sensory, motor, and association** areas. The combination of these three areas accounts for most of human cognition and behavior.

As teachers, we know the importance of including higher-order strategies in our daily assignments. We also know the importance of including social-emotional learning lessons in our units, morning meetings, assignments, classroom decor, everywhere!

Cerebellum

The cerebellum is found at the back of the brain and is divided into two hemispheres associated with each side of the body! So cool!

The cerebellum is in charge of:
- motor-learning
- sequence learning
- reflex memory
- judge distance
- coordination of voluntary movement
- balance

- posture
- emotional processing
- cognitive functions: language and attention

This is why movement integrated into lessons is so crucial. Our students' brains love and need movement. Gross and fine motor skills are always important to have in mind at the time of planning your lessons.

Fine motor skills are important for all students, big and small! This is a very random list of fine motor skills for toddlers, teens, adults, and ages in between! You know which ones are appropriate for your children! The point is to be intentional about incorporating fine motor skills no matter the subject or the age because the benefits are many: concentration, relaxation, problem-solving, decision making, and creativity.

- 3D puzzles
- beads onto a string
- biking
- bowling
- button and unbutton
- coloring
- drawing
- geoboards
- hand lettering
- handwriting
- Lego
- painting
- picking up small objects with the thumb and one finger
- playing an instrument
- puzzles
- Rubik's Cubes
- sewing

- stacking blocks
- stringing beads
- swimming
- turning pages of a book
- tying shoelaces
- use of rulers and other tools
- using scissors
- walking
- woodwork

Brain Stem

Your brainstem is the bottom part of your brain. It is a stem that connects your brain to your spinal cord. The brainstem sends signals to your body through the spinal cord. It controls your involuntary body functions such as your reflexes, heart rate, breathing, balance, and other thousands of things you need each second of your life!

So, try this with you and your class!

- please breathe deeply
- stand or sit while breathing
- draw your elbows back slightly to allow your chest to expand
- take a deep inhalation through your nose
- retain your breath for a count of five
- slowly release your breath by exhaling through your nose
- move, walk, or jump to get your heart moving too

There are so many other techniques for breathing… choose the one that works for you. Your brain and heart will thank you. Take a moment each day in your classroom to breathe deeply with your students!

Hippocampus

"The hippocampus plays a critical role in the formation, organization, and storage of new memories as well as connecting certain sensations and emotions to these memories" (Cherry, 2020). Have you ever gone to your grandparents' house and something you smell brings so many memories back? Thank your hippocampus!

The hippocampus is also in charge of spatial memory, memory consolidation, and memory transfer. As teachers, being aware of our students' spatial navigation or the ability to remember where an object is located or where an event occurred is very important. The hippocampus has an important role in long-term memory and for that, the hippocampus needs:

- music
- movement
- emotional links
- imagination
- mnemonics
- stories
- relevance
- love
- decluttered spaces
- smile
- novelty
- nature
- frequent breaks
- review
- reset
- reading
- games
- silence
- doodling

- art
- water
- sleep
- teaching to peers
- humor
- note-taking
- reflection
- thinking-out-loud
- goal-setting
- self-explaining
- balanced-instruction
- use of five senses
- and all the ideas and strategies that you have read in the previous chapters!

Amygdala

Understanding how the amygdala works is crucial for every educator. We need to provide a safe space for our students, otherwise, if they feel fear or threat, they will want to either fight, freeze, flee, or faint. When students feel fear and anxiety, memory and cognition are affected. We can't teach a fearful child. We need to take care of the anxiety and fear before we ask for any cognitive task.

This is what you can do in your classroom to avoid anxiety and fear in your students:

- use humor
- facilitate breathing exercises
- avoid punishments
- avoid fear-based strategies for classroom management
- use love-based strategies for classroom management
- avoid clipping students' behavior up and down on a chart

- avoid addressing a behavior publicly
- start the day with a morning relaxing ritual
- tell your students about what is coming in the lesson or day
- display a dual-coded agenda for the day (visual and text)
- talk about emotions
- use social-emotional lessons
- incorporate antiracist practices
- incorporate trauma-sensitive in everything you do
- provide a calm corner
- familiarize yourself with the effect of fear in your students' minds
- set a relaxing and loving tone
- invest time with each student
- get to know your student and what they like or don't like
- provide choice
- smile!

The Limbic Region

The limbic system, which is located deep within our brain, involves emotion and memory. One of the many functions of the limbic system is to record memories of experiences that left us with a positive or negative feeling or memory. This helps us avoid going through the same experiences by identifying threats and triggers. The limbic system, which includes the thalamus, hippocampus, and amygdala, helps us with the behaviors we need to survive.

The limbic region is known as the emotional brain. Our students' emotional brains can affect learning and memory. So, this is what you can do to support your student's limbic system:

- equip your students with tools to deal with stress and triggers
- co-regulate emotions with your students

- provide a calm corner or space with sensory tools, breathing techniques, strategies, and books that help your students regulate their emotions
- connect with your students beyond the academic relationship
- get to know them, what they like and fear
- show love and patience to your students

Neuroplasticity

Neuroplasticity brings educators so much hope. It means that our students can constantly learn new things, adapt to different experiences, and change the way they see and experience learning! Their brains can constantly change by what they learn, see, do, and feel at school, at home, or in any environment. This happens since the baby is formed in the uterus until we die.

Your students' brains are made up of billions of neurons. When students learn something new, their neurons make stronger connections. When you connect information to other information, through music, storytelling, emotions, movement, art, etc. the connection becomes stronger and so becomes the ability to remember what you teach!

Students need to be aware of the amazing benefits of neuroplasticity. You can explain this in simple words so they know what they can do for them. You can tell them that their first encounter with a new concept or skill may be hard, but as they keep making connections with the knowledge they already have, the connections become stronger and things can get easier with time, practice, and persistence! Make sure you help your students be in **awe** of what their brains can do for them!

Mirror Neurons

Have you noticed that when you smile at your students, many times they smile back? That is because of mirror neurons! "Mirror neurons are a type of brain cell that respond equally when we perform an action and when we witness someone else perform the same action" (Winerman, 2005, pg. 48). This is why we need to model the behaviors we hope to see in our students.

What should you model? Everything you believe your students need to learn.

- Model empathy.
- Model enthusiasm for learning.
- Model kindness.
- Model smiles.
- Model being in awe at our brains.
- Model writing.
- Model metacognition.
- Model self-explaining
- Model a great attitude to solve problems.
- Model healthy interactions.
- Model healthy habits.
- Model appropriate behavior.
- Model how to complete an assignment or activity.
- Model what high-quality work looks like.
- Model, model, model!

Whatever behaviors you wish to see in students, be the first to model them. While you're at it, model your enthusiasm and passion for teaching and learning. Because of this brain syncing, students unconsciously pick up on their teacher's mood, facial expressions, and actions far more than previously thought.

For a **fun unit that**
- **helps your students get to know their brains in a simple way**
- **and shows your students how they learn**

go to: https://yanina-s-school.thinkific.com/courses/brainfriendlyteacherbookresources

At the Brain-friendly Teacher Academy & Book Resources, you will also find many more resources to help you save time in your efforts to create lasting learning.

Enjoy!!!

Chapter 7: Brain-friendly Classroom Atmosphere & Classroom Management

Every time you enter an unfamiliar place, you look around and get a "vibe" from it. That place makes you feel and think a certain way about it and about you. Our students do the same when they enter a school building or your classroom. They get a sense if that place helps them feel at home, safe, seen, or not. Then, they form opinions about it. They decided if that place is familiar, friendly, safe, understanding, accepting, or not. Your classroom influences how your students feel about learning, about the physical space, and about you. As a result, their classroom atmosphere impacts negatively or positively on their academic performance.

Your classroom or learning space sends a message to your students even if you are not inside. They decide if they see themselves, if they feel seen, heard, respected, cherished, challenged, and loved. They make judgments about you, their learning space, and their learning experience according to the design, vibe, and atmosphere of their new classroom. The following are elements that need to be present in your classroom. They are a lot, and I am sure you know about all of them. I am sure you are already doing it. Take the following descriptions as a renewed invitation to be intentional about these things and as a reminder of how powerful they are for your students and you!

Sense of Safety

"Passion makes the world go 'round. Love just makes it a safer place." Ice-T

"Our brains are constantly registering information gathered from the physical environment, the emotional climate, and even the people around us to determine our level of safety at any given moment" (Jensen & McConchie, 2020). The amazing authors of the must-read book, Brain-based Learning, also say that "the three main areas of our brain's concern for our safety are our **physical** environment, our **emotional** environment, and our **social** environment."

Ideas for a safe environment:
- Create space for dialogue
- Smile
- Promote kindness
- Tell your students that you are a safe person to talk to if they feel not safe in the classroom or at school
- Check the temperature and lightning in the classroom
- Hold morning meetings
- Teach social-emotional skills
- Provide a calm corner
- Provide a place where they can express themselves creatively
- Commend a classmate each day or each week
- Ask students about their favorite color, music, artist, etc.
- Talk to each student
- Model vulnerability
- Have non-negotiables like bullying, name-calling, racism, etc.

Frequent Brain Breaks

"Taking a break can lead to breakthroughs." — *Russell Eric Dobda*

When students take brain breaks, brains are not idle, they are actually working "processing memories and making sense of experiences. The brain is not resting while at rest. The brain is working hard to create the memories and information needed to recall information just learned" (Barker, 2021).

Frequent breaks improve students' behavior, and capabilities to comprehend, imagine, be creative, stay motivated and come up with new ideas! It also reduces stress and cerebral congestion! Make sure you invite your students to move as much as possible. Movement doesn't cause misbehavior. The lack of movement many times leads to it! Brain breaks are good, but don't replace movement for brain breaks!!! Do both!!! Physical movement is the most transformative thing that can ever happen to us, teachers, and students!!!! See why:

Benefits of brain breaks:
- Breaks that involve movement improve physical and emotional health.
- Prevention of cognitive exhaustion.
- They restore motivation.
- Productivity and creativity.
- Consolidation of learning.
- Improve memory.
- Help renew strength to keep on working on an assignment.
- Give new perspectives.
- Improve humor.

Types of brain breaks:
- Ask your students to get up and do silly moves or just ask them to move around

- Play a game
- Have them work with their hands taking a cognitive break
- Take mental breaks
- Tell jokes
- Bring your students to nature or bring nature to the classroom
- Take a walk
- Daydream
- Brain dumps
- Get a healthy snack
- Breathing techniques
- Give the brain a break!

You can use brain breaks for transitions between classes. Resetting, though, can be used at the end of a long class or unit because we want our students to start fresh for the next lesson or unit!

Resetting

> *"Nothing in the universe can stop you from letting go and starting over."*
> -Guy Finley

New beginnings, resolutions, goals, classes, units, and semesters require a great deal of physical and mental strength. To start new and with renewed strength, **we need to reset!** Here are some ways for little and big humans to reset! Less screen time, more time in nature, meditation, playing music, decluttering your mind and physical spaces, reducing stress and artificial stimulant food, exercise, good sleep, reflection, focus on "being" before "doing."

Personally, I have a weekly reset and this has saved me physically, mentally, and spiritually. Each Friday night, I put all my things away: to-do lists, phone, computer, my regular books, everything that reminds me of my daily tasks. I spend my Sabbath, from the sunset on

Friday to the sunset on Saturday, in church, and nature, with my family, reading different things, and watching different things. I try to get things out of my mind during that day; it is hard sometimes, but because I am so used to doing this, I just have to switch to the thought that I get to do this once a week for my family, my physical, mental, and spiritual health and it works. On Sundays, I start the week seeing things from a different perspective. I feel renewed, recharged, and reset, ready to take on the week again. I have done this faithfully my whole life, and I know that this has helped me tremendously. Try it! Having a weekly Sabbath is proven to have huge benefits for our well-being!

Resetting allows your students and you to be more productive, creative, attentive, and focused. These are some ideas:

- Deep breathing
- Play a game
- Take a walk
- Reading
- Drawing & Doodling
- Dim lights
- Play calm music
- Tell jokes
- Set goals
- Move
- Brain breaks
- Coloring
- Take them out to nature
- Brain objects from nature to the classroom to use as manipulatives for math, science, reading, writing, etc.!
- Sensory breaks
- Allow quiet time or silence for those kiddos who need to reset to keep going.

Dialogue in the Classroom

"Dialogue is a lean language in which every word counts." - *Sol Stein*

We, teachers, need to provide the space and time for students to hold real dialogue. We are usually in a hurry and we do all the talking. When we allow students to engage in real instructional dialogue, they immerse in deep thought!

We want this!!! Here is how!
- provide the space and time for students to dialogue because students need to be seen and heard
- collaborative projects
- ask questions that require deep thinking
- discuss social issues & justice
- ask for solutions for different scenarios/problems
- provide time for reflection before dialogue
- think/pair/share
- debates
- teaching to peers
- "Learning is likely to be most effective when students are actively involved in the dialogic construction of meaning about topics that are of significance to them" (Wells and Arauz, 2006).

The Power of "We"

"Coming together is a beginning; keeping together is progress; working together is success." - *Edward Everett Hale.*

One of the greatest blessings I had as a mom and teacher was the fact that I taught both of my children at the school where I work. My daughter loved story time when she was in my classroom. She also liked that I enjoyed reading those books to her and her classmates. She would tell me many times that I was very dramatic while reading those stories!

One day, I was reading the same book to another class while she was walking in the hallway to go to her new classroom. She later asked me, "Mom, you were acting as if you never read that book before!!! You read it to my class and me, remember? You were so into that story and I know you know how that story ends!" To her surprise or disappointment, I answered, "When I read it to you, it was like my tenth time! I just think that if I show enthusiasm and all the feelings as I read it, my students will be into the story and enjoy reading books!"

Experts in the subject or not, we need to show enthusiasm to be co-learners with our students! At the time of starting a lesson, we can say, "We are going to learn about..." instead of "I will teach... and you will learn..." When we say "*us*," we are implying that we are going to experience learning **together** and that helps students realize that the lesson is relevant to their lives and ours.

Humor

"A day without laughter is a day wasted." - Charlie Chaplin

For some reason, I added humor and jokes during our virtual classes during the pandemic. My students loved it so much that I decided to include them in our in-person morning meetings now that we are back in our classrooms! That is one of the best decisions I have made as a teacher. The day I forget to read a joke from our age-appropriate joke book, they remind me! We all laugh about the good and bad jokes from that book! It helps me too to start the day relaxed and with a good laugh!

These are the benefits of using healthy humor in the classroom:

- eliminates boredom
- replaces tension and anxiety during classes with a relaxed atmosphere
- cognitive and psychological benefits
- maintains attention
- arouses the curiosity of students
- requests thinking
- attention and develop critical thinking
- promotes a positive environment
- encourages students to get out of patterns and try new approaches
- socialization
- strengthens the group dynamics
- therapeutic
- creates pleasant experiences

Ideas to use humor in your classroom:

- be funny at times
- add humorous items to tests
- add humorous notes to homework
- add humorous notes to class assignments.
- display humor quotes
- keep a cartoon file
- have joke days
- ask students to add humor to writing assignments
- ask students to bring in books they think are funny
- avoid "hurt" humor & sarcasm
- use only healthy humor
- ask your students for ideas to bring healthy humor to their classroom
- laugh/smile during morning meeting

- read humorous picture books
- add humorous images to assignments
- display humor quotes
- ready funny poetry
- use tongue twisters
- have a joke log
- use different funny voices
- bring humorous t-shirts if they are allowed at your school!
- tell funny stories about yourself!
- wear silly sunglasses to welcome your students
- wear a silly hat
- approach your and your students' mistakes with a sense of humor
- wear a smile as much as you can!

Aromas

"I truly do feel like scent can change your mood and the feeling in a room."
- Tish Cyrus

In a study about aromas, cognition, and mood done by Moss, Mark, Hewitt, Steven, Moss, Lucy, and Wesnes, Keith in 2008 at the Northumbria University, they discovered that peppermint was found to enhance memory. These results supported the idea that aromas of essential oils can produce significant and idiosyncratic effects on both subjective and objective assessments of aspects of human behavior.

Check with your students and their parents first for allergies before bringing an essential oil diffuser. You can always bring plants and herbs with aromas too. Natural aromas are always better!

Fresh Air

"Some old-fashioned things like fresh air and sunshine are hard to beat."
- *Laura Ingalls Wilder*

There is nothing better than going outside for recess to get fresh air. But, we don't have to wait until go out to enjoy the fresh air. Open those classroom windows if you can while your students are learning. Let that fresh air run free in your classroom!

Benefits of fresh air:
- higher levels of oxygen
- clear the lungs
- boost in the immune system
- more clarity to the brain
- clear thinking
- focus
- concentration
- improvement of blood pressure
- better mood
- energy
- break for the mind
- decrease of cognitive load
- better digestion
- sharper mind

Students in stuffier classrooms did worse on standardized tests than did students in buildings with fresher air" (Landhuis, 2015). So, open those windows, bring plants to your classroom, and hold classes outside. Your brain and your students' brains will thank you! Cognition improves with fresh air! Win-win!

Plants

"Plants give us oxygen for the lungs and for the soul." — Terri Guillemets

I am not a plant lady (yet!). But, I do have one plant in our classroom. One of my students' moms gave it to us! We even named it. It is called "Mr. Photosynthesis!" I know, very original! We love our plant and I think this plant loves us too. He is growing amazingly fast and beautiful. "Mr. Photosynthesis" is part of our classroom family! I wish I had more plants, but I need to make sure I can keep this one alive for many years so I can be confident that I can have more!

"Indoor plants have been linked to improved concentration and memory as well as a stress reduction. Research has also linked indoor plants with increased productivity and reduced mental fatigue (Dabbs, 2019). Plants not only bring cognitive benefits but emotional ones. Students love being responsible for taking care of nature.

If you are a plant person, you have all my admiration. If you are not, start with a cactus or one small plant!

Silence

"Listen to silence. It has so much to say." – Rumi

You read about the importance of instructional conversations in the classroom, about dialogue, asking questions, working in groups, and so many other things that require talking, not silence. But, as we know, there is a place, space, *and need* for everything. You know when your students need to enjoy silence in order to focus on the certain acquisition of concepts and skills. And for that, you need to provide the space and time for that to happen! We can't expect a classroom to be in silence for hours and hours, but we can help them enjoy silence for some periods at a time, depending on your students' age.

"When we allow students time to attend to their own thoughts, students can develop a better understanding of themselves and their work," says a study in The Cambridge Journal of Education cited by Phillips (2018).

Silence can be used to:

- Add some suspense to a lecture, lesson, or activity
- Provide students the space and time to think by themselves
- Listen to our own thoughts
- Enjoy the learning or thinking process
- Practice metacognition
- Practice self-explaining
- Reflect
- Be creative
- Allow time and space to focus
- Enjoy relaxation and calm
- Give a break to introverted students

I know that silence can be awkward at the beginning, but you don't have to ask for silence from your students for long periods of time. Start with a few minutes per day during activities that demand focus and attention.

After all, there is such a thing as "noise pollution!" Students can't focus if there is constant talking, constant background music, and constant outside noise. Try to provide silence when you can. Students are constantly hearing our directions, their classmates, music, and hallway noise. Silence can also calm our racing thoughts and anxiety.

You can start by incorporating the following as you see fit; you can do one of these things once a day or once a week. Try it and see what happens!

- Silent reading
- Silent writing
- Silent coloring
- Silent doodling
- Silent review: students write what they learned in a journal

Teacher Reflection

"Reflective thinking turns experience into insight." - John C. Maxwell.

Do you reflect on your day on your way home? I know that some days you are like, "Oh, that lesson did so well! I am repeating it next year!" Or, "Oh, that lesson was a disaster! I am never doing it again!" That is an honest reflection and we teachers do it automatically! The key is to write important reflections under your planning or somewhere secure so you can remember what to do next time you teach that lesson or unit!

"When instructors engage in reflective teaching, they are dedicating time to evaluate their own teaching practice, examine their curricular choices, consider student feedback, and make revisions to improve student belonging and learning" (Yale Poorvu Center for Teaching and Learning).

We believe that students' self-assessment is powerful and so it is for us teachers. I know it takes even more time for us. You can have a system that works for you like:

- Daily or weekly journals
- Videos

- Rubrics
- Student response
- Portfolio
- Peer assessment
- Student evaluation, which can be rated by emojis!
- Blog about your lesson
- Leave a space on your digital or paper planner to write briefly how your lesson or unit went and what you can change next time you teach the same, or even when your students "aha" moment!

Don't say "It is easy!"

"There will be obstacles. There will be doubters. There will be mistakes. But with hard work, there are no limits." - Michael Phelps.

As a child, every time I heard, "This is so easy," from my teachers and classmates, I always wondered what was wrong with me because nothing has come and will come easy to me. I had fairly good grades, but it never came easy, never!

So, let's try to avoid saying these words and encourage our students to use other words instead, so other learners don't feel there is something wrong with them. This applies to so many aspects of life, not just when it comes to learning.

What can we say instead?
- It is not easy yet. It will get easier with practice.
- This might seem hard at first, but I believe you can do it.
- You might not get it right the first time.
- It will come with practice, you will see!
- This is hard, but we will approach it one step at a time!

What students can say:
- "I have practiced this before"
- "I struggled with math word problems, but I have practiced a lot and I can get it now"
- "I still need to practice more on this"

Student Goals

"My personal goals are to be happy, healthy, and to be surrounded by loved ones."
- Kiana Tom

Motivation is an internal force that allows students to have and pursue goals. We can inspire and encourage up to a certain degree. The student is the ultimate one who carries through. "As teachers, we're tasked with helping students find their own motivation, leading them to suitable goals, and lighting the path to get there" (Williams, 2019).

Motivation, among many other things, can help students set short and long-term goals. We as teachers can help our students set and reach individual goals. Each student, though, needs to set personalized goals when it comes to academics, physical, social, mental, and spiritual goals.

Goals help students stay focused, have a map, be on-task, and be motivated! When goals are reached, students feel accomplished and ready to set bigger goals! Goals are like writing the exact destination on your phone! When you **write** the exact address on the GPS, you know **where** you need to be, **why** you want/need to go, and finally, the GPS tells you **how** by marking you each turn!

"There is a tried-and-true piece of advice that your long-term, milestone, and process goals will be more motivating if they are SMART: Specific, Measurable, Ambitious, Realistic, and Time-limited

(Doran, 1981). In other words, you should be concrete about each goal and ensure that you can measure progress and attainment. Goals need to be balanced for your students, not too hard, and not too easy. That is why goals need to be individualized for or by each student.

Tips for goal making:

- Provide different categories for goal setting: for each subject, study skills, short-term, long terms
- Help them see their target destinations according to their strengths and weaknesses
- Help your students have a point of departure and arrival
- Write those goals and adjust them as you accomplish them
- Students can also write goals for other aspects of their life: spiritual, physical, financial, relational, social, professional, and mental

What goals do *you* have as a teacher, mom, dad, or human? Let's inspire our students to write their goals too!

Breathing in the classroom

"The wisest one-word sentence? Breathe." – Terri Guillemets

We, teachers, are in a rush every single minute of the school day that I think, sometimes, we forget to breathe deeply. Does this happen to you too? Right now, why don't you stop reading this and take ten deep breaths? It feels good, right?

Deep breathing in the classroom:
- reduces anxiety
- relaxes the body
- quiets the mind

- increases students' academic success
- helps students manage time
- controls addictions and cravings
- reduces stress and enhances sleep
- achieves athletic success and body satisfaction
- enhances the immune system
- develops a deeper sense of compassion for others and self
- calms our minds
- forces us to stop
- helps us reset
- helps us to start again
- increases motivation to continue an assignment
- helps us see a bigger picture
- stops our racing minds
- helps our students be graceful to their friends and themselves

Non-verbal communication

"Listen with your eyes as well as your ears." — *Graham Speechley*

Have you ever heard people say something to you verbally and say something totally different through their non-verbal communication? It is kind of off, right? Well, we need to be aware that we don't do that to our students unintentionally! Some of the components of nonverbal communication that are helpful in the classroom are:

- facial expression
- body movements
- smiles
- tone of voice
- eye contact
- gestures

Let's be aware and intentional about nonverbal communication because many times, these things communicate stronger than words.

Eye Contact

"Eye contact beats any conversation." - Christina Strigas

Eye contact is a powerful way to show that we really care about our students. Things to consider about eye contact in the classroom according to Ledbury (2014):

- Welcome your students by saying their names and looking into their eyes.
- Talk to your learners, not to the book, the board, or the screen.
- Eyes can set the tone of a lesson.
- Good eye contact does not mean staring or gazing. Many learners are likely to find this uncomfortable.
- Monitor their eyes. They usually can tell if they are bored, anxious, excited, etc.
- Encourage your learners to make eye contact while they are working together in pairs or groups.
- The more eye contact, the more engagement, and participation!
- Look at your students' eyes when praising them.

Other great things that come from eye contact:
- The child receives the message/instruction/encouragement more clearly.
- It builds confidence in the child.
- Eye contact makes your words more memorable.
- It helps students concentrate more when you look into their eyes.

- It makes you more likable.
- They remember better what you say.
- You build a deeper connection.
- Some cultures avoid eye contact and we need to be aware of that!

Eye-level conversations

Bending down to talk to children has more benefits than we think!
- Children feel safer.
- They feel more in control.
- They feel more connected to us.
- We let them know that we are there for them.
- It shows that we are paying attention to them.
- By looking them eye to eye, you are catching the attention of your student.
- The student is more likely to be able to absorb what is told.
- It is also less intimidating than if the adult is talking down to them.
- It builds empathy.

Trauma-informed practices

"A trauma-informed classroom recognizes that kids have gone through some serious events in their lives. Not only do they carry the memory of those events with them, but their brains are different because of this trauma." - Kenton Levings

"Up to two-thirds of U.S. children have experienced at least one type of serious childhood trauma, such as abuse, neglect, natural disaster, or experiencing or witnessing violence. (CDC, 2019). Students who experience trauma have difficulty with self-regulation, negative thinking, and trusting adults. Teachers may not understand the root of this behavior, "which can lead to misunderstandings, ineffective interventions, and missed learning time" (Minahan, 2019).

I am so glad that there is so much information about this for teachers. These are just some things you can start using in your classroom as you start being a more trauma-sensitive and informed teacher:

- Build relationships with each one of your students
- Spend time with each student, at least a few minutes per week
- Create a safe classroom atmosphere
- Look beyond the behavior
- There is no need to ask personal questions
- Create routines
- Teach students breathing techniques
- Provide a time-in corner (not for time out)
- Have routines and rituals
- Get familiarized with how the brain works when it is in fear
- Be consistent
- De-escalate
- Co-regulate
- Teach self-regulation skills
- Listen more and talk less
- Try not to take students' reactions personally
- Share your expectations
- Offer support
- Eliminate fear-based classroom management
- Teach social-emotional skills
- Check your own emotions and reactions
- Give students the time and space to talk and write about their feelings, experiences, thoughts, etc.
- Remind yourself that behavior is a form of communication.
- Make sure your teaching is culturally responsive!

Embrace students' diversity

"Strength lies in differences, not in similarities" by Stephen R. Covey.

Dr. Zaretta Hammond, in her book, Culturally Responsive Teaching & The Brain, defines "culturally responsive teaching simply as an educator's ability to recognize students' cultural displays of learning and meaning-making and respond positively and constructively with teaching moves that use cultural knowledge as a scaffold to connect what the student knows to new concepts" (2015, pg. 15).

Culture is the lens that our students use to see and understand the world. Each family has its own culture, regardless of nationality, ethnicity, race, and language. That means that we have so many cultures represented in our classroom. Students need to see their culture and their classmates' culture in their textbooks, wall décor, music, art, and assignments.

Ideas to acknowledge your students' culture:
- Celebrate each of your students' culture
- Get to know each one of your students
- Connect with their parents
- Show and tell about their culture
- Ask them to write about their traditions, faith, food, spirituality, etc., and share with the class if they feel comfortable
- Talk about the importance of accepting everyone.
- Make sure you have library books and textbooks that represent many cultures
- Talk about the dangers of stereotyping
- Be open and talk against racism
- Be anti-racist
- Check your bias
- Don't ignore race

- Be willing to unlearn and unpack your belief systems
- Be willing to learn
- Study the difference between your intentions and your impact
- Be a lifelong learner of these topics
- Talk about social justice
- Listen to them and try to see how they see the world
- As a teacher, inform yourself about how to be more culturally responsive
- Show and teach about tolerance
- Be authentically interested in each one of your students.

No more "raise your hands."

"Never be afraid to speak your mind, you have one for a reason."
— Sarah Moores.

When we ask students to raise their hands, the following might happen:

- Not all students participate.
- After one student answers, the others shut down.
- The same students raise their hands every time.
- We never have 100% participation.
- Students are afraid of being wrong, and they don't raise their hands.
- It is only effective for the quickest thinkers.
- As soon as one hand goes up, everyone else stops thinking.

What to do instead!
- Choral response
- Catch-release, whisper the answer into their hands, and hold it there; they all release the answer!
- Turn and talk
- Write and reveal

- Point to the answer
- Use whiteboards
- Use any online app that picks names randomly
- Thumbs up/Thumbs down for yes or no
- Call on students randomly
- Thumb to the chest if they have an idea, two fingers to their chest if they have two ideas or more
- Think-pair-share
- Use popsicle sticks with the students' names written on them.
- Have students share the answer with the student next to them.
- Have students answer on individual whiteboards.
- Have students answer "yes" or "no" using sign language.
- Have students answer multiple-choice questions with sign language letters: a, b, c, and d.
- After you have called on a student, ask other students if they agree or disagree and why.
- Give students a sticky note when they walk into the classroom and instruct them to write down their questions or comments and hand them to you after class or when you are not talking.

Uniqueness

"There is immense power when a group of people with similar interests gets together to work toward the same goals." – Idowu Koyenikan

Find something that your class enjoys as a group and use it in your meetings and instruction! Is there something that your class likes such as a song, a special book, or an inside joke? Use **that** in your classroom, home, emails, or mail. Your students will feel they are part of something special! This is crucial even if you meet every day at school because it sends your students a message of community, a welcoming atmosphere, and togetherness.

Visual Displays

"I believe in a visual language that should be as strong as the written word."
- David LaChapelle

Remember that the way you decorate your classroom, more specifically what you display on your walls, impact your students' behavior and academic performance. These are the do(s) and don'ts of visuals in the classroom:

Do:
- Display student work
- Display student work at eye level
- Bring display to a minimum
- Play with lights
- Avoid clutter
- Add the minimum graphics to worksheets
- Balance wall colors
- Leave a blank space
- Use visual aids
- Leave space around the posters
- Keep your posters and anchor charts current
- Have your students create their own anchor charts
- Have your students give you input about décor, functionality, anchor charts, and how they want their work displayed

Don't:
- Cover all the walls with displays
- Add so many things to worksheets
- Have all the walls with bright colors
- Fill your room with unnecessary décor
- Decorate your whole room with content that is not relevant to your students' current unit
- Fall into the trap of following decoration trends

Building anticipation

"The idea of waiting for something makes it more exciting" — Andy Warhol

Building anticipation releases the same or more dopamine than the actual event or experience! So, build anticipation before school starts, before teaching a new unit, before a special thing that will happen in your classroom by putting notes on their desks or sending a postcard, video, email, or text!

Examples:
- "Bring a towel tomorrow!" (for an ocean unit)
- "Enter our room very silently tomorrow!"
- Distribute invitations for an upcoming event!

Interest Inventory

"To be interesting, be interested." — Dale Carnegie

Each year I send a questionnaire with about 20 questions to each one of my students on the first day of school or in the mail before school starts. Along with that questionnaire, I respond to each one of my students so they can get to know me on a human level, as someone who loves cheesecakes and chocolate! It doesn't matter when you do it, as long as you do it to get to know your students better!

After you have the inventory, you can tailor your projects, writing prompts, field trips, lectures, presentations, objects for hooks, and so much more. Students will feel seen and heard. Even if you can't have everything they like in your classroom, the mere fact of being interested in them and asking them about their hobbies and favorite things will mean more than you know to your students.

Judging Trends on social media

"The thing is to be able to outlast the trends." - Paul Anka

Let me make a parenthesis here and talk about trends or trains on which we unnecessarily jump when we scroll on social media. Many times we think that trends can be a good thing for our classroom design, instruction, or even classroom atmosphere. It can be a good thing or it can't. It can be good, but not necessarily great for our students' learning experience. When you scroll on social media and see something cool, judge if having that shiny object will contribute to your students' meaning and lasting learning experience. If not, please don't buy it. You will waste money and trends just pass!

Also, when you see a cute digital product to use with your students, judge if your students can do it using pencil and paper and have the same meaningful and lasting learning experience. The same goes when we see that other teachers got some cute things for one or less than a dollar. Then, we buy all the things even if they cost more than one dollar! So we end up spending a lot of money on just "cute" things, thinking that we will give an excellent use for them, but then it just stands on bookshelves. I am guilty of this.

So, when we bring something cute just for the sake of cuteness, it just adds clutter to our classroom, atmosphere, and instruction. As a result, it ends up cluttering our students' minds as well. Plain worksheets and functional classroom design can help your students focus better. Our students need less in their classroom space, less in worksheets, less busy work, and less digital busywork. Less is better for your students' brains.

We don't need to follow trends to be great teachers. The old ways that work are still powerful. Many new things are great too. Just be wise to judge trends and see if they really benefit your students. You are a fantastic teacher, and you know best what works for your students!

Choice

"If you choose not to decide, you still have made a choice." - Neil Peart.

Choice. What a beautiful word! We love having choices as a teacher as to how to teach our students content and standards in the best way possible. We tend to dislike scripted curriculums because we want to choose better resources for a better learning experience.

Our students like the word "choice" too. Just as we teachers can't choose 100% how to teach a lesson, students don't have the opportunity either to choose 100% how to learn a lesson or how to show evidence as to how well they learned it. But, as much as possible and when we see fit, we can provide choice to our students! They will appreciate this gesture! "Everything in class is not a choice, but there are many opportunities to offer student choice in the classroom" (Parker, Novak, and Bartell, 2017).

When teachers get to choose absolutely everything for their students, their motivation decrease, and they feel like they need to fight for their rights to choose in one way or another! They need the opportunity to choose in order to solve problems, think independently, and use their imagination and creativity!

When you give your students age-appropriate choices, they are motivated, and they thrive on trying and learning new things. More about choice in the classroom:

- Provide a student choice board for students who have finished their assignments.
- Give them a choice of how you want them to show you evidence of learning.
- Give them the time and space daily or weekly to write based on their interests.
- Give them the time and space daily or weekly to read books based on their interests.

Spontaneity

"Only in spontaneity can we be who we truly are." - John McLaughlin

From the minute your students arrive in your classroom, they know they need to follow a schedule, a routine, and rituals. This is beautiful and necessary. But don't forget to leave some buffer time for "spontaneity" in your classroom! We have packed schedules, and there is no time for free or "spontaneity" time, yet this is crucial for your students.

Free play and spontaneity in the classroom benefit executive functions! This is totally a win-win! I know it is hard to just take time from our busy schedule. I know we have exact minutes for each class and can never afford to waste time. But try to see where you can provide "unstructured" minutes to explore a concept or a skill. Imagine students being more attentive after this "unstructured" time!

Have you tried one of these things?
- Provide free time to play: structured games are fantastic, but they do not replace free play!
- free time to write - creative writing
- free time to read what they want

- a genius hour where students choose what to investigate, do, construct, etc.
- the choice to show how and what they have learned
- free time to reflect and write about what they have learned or experienced at school
- time and space for calm time
- more contact with nature

Benefits of free time
- creativity
- relaxation
- enhances cognitive functions
- improves behavior and social skills
- improves long-term memory
- improves problem-solving skills
- emotional balance
- self-regulation

Harms of not having downtime:
- anxiety
- poor resilience
- depression
- cognitive load
- overwhelm

Let Students Work Together

"No two minds ever come together without, thereby, creating a third, invisible, intangible force which may be likened to a third mind." — Napoleon Hill

Every time I announce in my classroom that they can work in groups, they get so excited! Of course, they are very social so I have to revise some boundaries so they can get some work done! I did also have students who didn't get so excited about working in groups, but after they experienced working in groups, they felt better about it and wanted to do it again!

Working together can be messy, loud, and even disorganized... but is not this exactly how we work with other adults in the real world? When working in groups hard conversations and disagreements take place but don't give up and model healthy conflict resolutions. The results will be worth it for you and your students.

Benefits of working in groups:

- Face-to-face interactions such as smiling and eye contact
- Students get a good feeling as a result of helping each other
- Students are part of something bigger than themselves
- The group has a shared goal in mind
- Group members need to listen, make decisions together, trust each other and solve problems

Just Time

"The two most powerful warriors are patience and time." – *Leo Tolstoy*

Sometimes there is nothing wrong with our students or their pace to learn something. Sometimes it is just a matter of time and being patient with each child's learning process. "Giving students substantial time during class to pause, reflect on, and verbally process their understanding can help them consolidate their learning and generate new ideas," says Tina Grotzer, from the Harvard Graduate School of Education. Berman and colleagues (2008) suggest that "breaks and time to reflect can be cognitively restorative"

In a culture and time where we want instant solutions, we think automatically that there is something wrong with us as teachers or with students when they have a hard time learning something new. Before feeling hopeless, frustrated, or jumping to conclusions, let's try giving the precious gift of time!

Also, as a teacher, I was afraid of things that I thought I couldn't do right, but time was exactly what I needed! Giving time to learn a skill is hard when we are always in a rush to cover all the curriculum. It requires a lot of patience and grace, but it is so worth it! So, try time!

Embrace Mistakes

"Making mistakes is a lot better than not doing anything."
- Billie Joe Armstrong

One of the first things I say when I have a new class and new students is, "It is OK to make mistakes in this class. We actually embrace and welcome mistakes because they help us learn too!" Then, we proceed to play games that require a lot of tries and a lot of errors. That way, they don't enter my classroom having to come up right away with exact answers. In that process, I get to know my students and give them feedback that sets the tone for embracing mistakes, learning from them, and discussing them with actual smiles!

Mistakes are an important part of the process of learning. We need to make sure that our students are OK with making and welcoming mistakes in order to experience amazing things! Take the case of Edison, Michael Jordan, Vincent van Gogh, Mozart, Ford, Newton, Monet, the Wright brothers, and thousands more who made mistakes and as a result, they became better at what they were doing. So much better that they made history!

I know that as teachers; we are OK with our students making mistakes, but let's be intentional about letting them know that mistakes are welcome and necessary for authentic learning! Let's give them examples of people who have made mistakes before they intended something amazing. Finally, let's give them the time and space to do things that require trial and error: like open-ended solutions to problems, and the opportunity to show evidence of learning in different ways that require their creativity and mistakes!

Focused Work

"Focus on the journey, not the destination. Joy is found not in finishing an activity but in doing it." - Greg Anderson.

Provide time and space for you and your students to be able to focus and get things done! Cal Newport, the author of the book "Deep Work", writes about priming the environment for deep and focused work.

Ways to prime the classroom for focused work:
- Minimize distractions
- Make sure your students have water available
- Check that the temperature is pleasant
- Take out of the way things that are not needed for the lesson
- Leave at hand only the things you need for a lesson

Talk to your students about
- Build stamina, start focused work little by little, and increase the time without interrupting it. Don't ask too much time of yourself.
- Getting up and moving frequently and getting back to focused work
- Drinking water

- Sleeping well
- Spending time in nature
- Avoiding multitasking
- Enjoying the moment
- Trying to avoid distractions
- Practicing staying in silence

Prime Time

"Until we can manage time, we can manage nothing else." - Peter Drucker

When is your prime time to read a book, work out, write, answer emails, and teach or learn a certain lesson? "Your "biological prime time" is the time of the day when you have the most energy and, therefore, the greatest potential to be productive" (Bailey, 2013).

What subject do you teach first? Your students' biological prime time is the time of the day when they have the most energy. How do you use that time?! Remember that you, too, have a biological prime time! So, don't force your body to do something during a time when you feel tired or like resting. Listen to your body and if you can help it, design your classroom daily schedule around your students' prime time.

Awe

"When I look at the human brain, I'm still in awe of it." - Ben Carson

Do you stop to smell the flowers? Are you in awe of the little things? Are we too busy to live in **awe**? "If a child is to keep alive, his inborn sense of wonder... he needs the companionship of at least one adult who can share it, rediscovering with him the joy, excitement, and mystery of the world we live in" (Carson, 1998).

Ideas to bring "awe" to your classroom:

- Invite your students to pay attention to the "littlest" creatures, patterns, and ordinary things in nature. For example, you can bring binoculars and magnifying lenses for a walk outside.
- Look through your students' eyes and be **in awe** as well. If they are not in awe, model (say what you see, smell, feel) the sense of wonder for them: when you read a story, learn a new math skill, take a walk, sing a song, read a poem, go back to history, etc. Live in awe for them and you!
- Give them time and space to enjoy a piece of art or grass!
- Ask yourself in front of your students, "I wonder why..." and then invite them to write or talk about the things they wonder about!

Uncluttered Space

"Outer order contributes to inner calm." —Gretchen Rubin

We tend to put all the things on classroom walls: artwork, student work, maps, anchor charts, decoration, bulletin boards, borders for bulletin boards, and so many more things. Cluttered spaces and too much decoration on walls disrupt the attention of students. **Less** (on walls, surfaces, tables, bookshelves) **is more** for attention, learning, and behavior!

Tips for decluttering the surfaces of bookshelves, desktops, and tables!

Bookshelves

- leave the surface as empty as possible
- take everything off
- wipe it up
- put only what is extremely necessary for learning
- take unnecessary decor out too

Teacher desk or kidney tables
- Have a tilted desk for your computer, so you avoid a flat surface to put so many things on it.
- Do you use only one pen? Just leave that one!
- Put everything else in bins. The clear ones also seem to show clutter.
- Label those bins and leave them close if you need those things daily.
- Assign a place for the few things you need.

Declutter corners and floor too. Do you want to go even further? Take out some furniture that is holding unnecessary stuff, and you won't have to worry about decluttering it.

Uncluttered student space

A good system shortens the road to the goal. ~ Orison Swett Marden

- Reserve a weekly time for students to clean their desks.
- Assign spaces for different things, so each thing has its place.
- Use containers.
- Graded papers need to go home!
- If there are things they don't use in the classroom, they can take them home.
- Invite them to come up with a system that works!
- Model, model, model with your own space!

Habits and Rituals

"Watch your thoughts, they become your words; watch your words, they become your actions; watch your actions, they become your habits; watch your habits, they become your character; watch your character, it becomes your destiny."
- Lao Tzu.

Habits and rituals are different things, and both are necessary for the classroom. Habits are lining up, putting books away, morning meetings, greetings, dismissals, cleaning, etc. Rituals are how uniquely your students perform each habit in your classroom! Make sure you add a special or silly ritual to each habit!

- Lining up: choose a special song for it!
- Putting books away: what can be a special way of doing this?
- Morning meeting: special songs, jokes, something unique that your class likes.
- Greetings: greet students according to their choices.
- Dismissals: choose your special routine.
- Cleaning: play a special and unique song that your class loves.

Habit is what you do, and rituals are how you do it. Rituals can be amazing for your class. They can vote on how they would like to do it. This will bring a sense of community and uniqueness!

Transitions

"Your life is a story of transition. You are always leaving one chapter behind while moving on to the next." – Anonymous

Transitions help set the tone for the next learning experience. Transitions are not only used for quick and effective change from one class to another. They are a powerful tool to engage/energize, focus, and calm students' brains, which are different states required for different kinds of activities or learning experiences.

Make them fun, calm, or engaging according to the needs of your students' brains and based on the previous and next class! All the following strategies can be timed according to your schedule. Always leave a tiny buffer in your lesson plan so your students can rest from the cognition load they had and to prepare them for what is coming!!!

We can't hold weight without stopping and resting. Our brains need precisely the same thing! The following are tips for "quick and smooth" transitions between classes/subjects!

Try this:
- play sounds (or a bell) and ask students to do a certain thing when they hear that
- a quick reflection on journals
- movement or short recess
- doodling or art
- academic conversations with partners
- call and response phrases
- brain dumps on paper or talk to a friend
- exit tickets
- tell jokes
- play a song
- allow daydreaming
- read a mini-story
- have them draw what they learned
- breathing exercises or brain breaks or silence time
- much better if it includes movement
- puzzles
- drink water
- play with nature objects

Joy

"A wise teacher makes learning a joy" - King Salomon (Proverbs 15: 2)

This quote comes from the wisest person on this planet. I am sure there must be so many reasons behind the need to make learning a joy! Have you ever felt a knot in your stomach knowing you had to attend a certain class? I have and I don't want that for my students. I want them to come to my classroom with joy because they know that they are going to find joy in it! There are times when we will go through situations that are not so joyful, but after that situation or feelings go away, we know that we will come back to that usual state soon!

I like the definition of joyful learning by Opitz & Ford (2014), "We define joyful learning as acquiring knowledge or skills in ways that cause pleasure and happiness. Recently, the focus has been on the first half of that definition, e.g. knowledge or skills, to the exclusion of the second half, e.g. pleasure and happiness (pg. 10).

Joy in the classroom:

- decreases stress
- decreases anxiety
- helps students wanting to come to their classroom each day
- fosters community
- depends a lot on the teacher's attitude and enthusiasm for teaching, the school, the classroom, the class
- helps students be ready to learn
- helps students feel they belong
- provides a sense of safety and acceptance

Brain-friendly Classroom Atmosphere & Classroom Management

Ways to bring joy to the classroom!

- show a smile when a student calls your name
- show a smile while teaching
- show a smile while giving feedback
- show excitement as you and your students are learning something new
- tell jokes
- add humor to assignments or tests
- laugh at jokes
- play with your students
- give students choice
- find pleasure in learning
- read pleasant books
- let students teach
- let students be silly
- play happy music
- play silly music
- sing silly songs
- by silly at times
- let students be themselves
- remember that you are teaching children
- show your human side
- provide a safe learning environment
- share your story
- share mistakes you made

And now, the last brain-friendly "strategy!"

Love

"Love doesn't make the world go 'round. It's what makes the ride worthwhile"
Franklin P. Jones

Yes, love! I know you love your students. It is hard not to when we spend so many hours a day, days a week, and months of the year with them. But, we are so busy that we might not intentionally show them that. Love makes the classroom atmosphere complete!

This is how you can show appropriate affection to your students:

- Make eye contact while smiling.
- Make time to talk for a few minutes with each one of your students.
- Leave individual notes of appreciation for each one of your students.
- Be present when they come to ask you things and tell you stories.
- Show interest in their hobbies.
- Be sensitive to their needs and emotions.
- Tell your students something special and unique about them.
- Greet your students with a smile.
- Dismiss your students with a smile and a word of appreciation and encouragement.

"And the greatest of these is Love."
(1 Corinthians 13:13)

The End

My Teacher Smiles

After so many strategies, tips, and research, you might feel overwhelmed or think that you have to do all this to be a great teacher. I am here to tell you that you already are. The mere fact of picking this book and making it to the end means that you want to grow as a teacher, that you care about your students, that you love what you do, even if (or when) it is hard.

This book is not a recipe for teaching; it is a book full of strategies that you can pick and choose. A bank of simple research-based strategies that do not require a lot of money and resources to implement. Oftentimes, effective strategies are the ones that are not fancy and shiny! Oftentimes, the old strategies, pencil, and paper are the most meaningful to students! I am here to tell you that you are doing it right. You have been doing it right because there is no other teacher who knows your students better than you do. You know how they learn best! So, use this book as a reference to get more ideas, to be assured that simple and easy instructional strategies, classroom design, and atmosphere tips can make a huge difference in your students!

I am not saying goodbye, because I know you will leave this reference book at your teacher's desk, by your planner or computer… but I want to end this book with a shocking moment I had after coming back to my classroom.

I needed to go to a professional development event, so I asked a sub to come to my classroom the next day. I left all the regular assignments, plus a worksheet where they had to describe me because their teacher "went missing." That day I was gone, I often wondered what my students thought about me! I was sure that they were going to say that they loved their classroom setting and the amazing instructional strategies that I use to make sure they have a meaningful and lasting learning experience. I do try to put into practice what I write in this book! Some days I do it better than others!!!! I will never tell you that I follow all these strategies every single minute of the day. I lean into them. I try to be intentional about classroom design, instructional strategies, and an atmosphere that engage, focus, and calm my students' brains.

So, with all of this in mind, I was sure that I was coming to see my students' notes showing how they appreciated doing hexagonal thinking, doodling while listening to audio stories, and all the fun things they do to remember what they learn!

Well, that is not how they described me! Some said those things, but all of them wrote these two things about me:

"My teacher smiles and likes apple pie!"

I was in shock when I realized what they all had in common. They described me as a person and not so much as their teacher!!!!!!!!!!!! Since that day, I kept reflecting on those two things they all wrote about me, seriously! I have been trying to decode what that **really** means to me.

I invite you to try as well and find a message! This is what it still means to me after so many years: they see me as a person and they see my smile. They appreciate and like my smile. They like when their teacher smiles. From that moment on, I smiled even more, and while doing that, I realized that my smile might have made my brain-friendly classroom design, instructional strategies, and classroom atmosphere even better and more effective!

I invite you to **breathe deeply and show a smile** to your students every day!

About the Author

Yanina is a happy wife, mom, teacher, speaker, researcher, and writer. She is currently working on her Ph.D. She loves sharing brain-friendly tips for classroom design, instruction, and classroom atmosphere on her Brain-friendly Teacher Academy.

Brain-friendly Teacher Academy is a platform where she shares professional development videos and resources for free, so teachers from around the globe can access it to transform their teaching practices and their students' learning experiences:
https://yanina-s-school.thinkific.com/courses/**SendMeBraintips**

This academy has a special place for this book, where you will find the resources to take the information on this book to the next level in your classroom:
https://yanina-s-school.thinkific.com/courses/**BrainFriendlyTeacherBookResources**

She also loves connecting with other teachers on social media while constantly sharing her research in practical tips to be used right away in your classroom.

Instagram: https://instagram.com/lets.celebrate.learning
Facebook Group: facebook.com/groups/braintipsforyourclassroom
Podcast: Science of Learning

Yanina loves Jesus, her family, nature, traveling, fruit tarts, her many animals at her farm in Illinois, and her multi-grade classroom family! More here: https://**BrainFriendlyTeacher**.wordpress.com/

Let's Connect!

First off, if you liked this book, would you leave a review on Amazon? Thank you!

Brain-friendly Teacher Academy & Book Resources

https://yanina-s-school.thinkific.com/courses/brainfriendlyteacherbookresources

Did you like this book? Then, you will love this place where you can take your desire to be a friend-friendly teacher to another level! Go now to get:
- a classroom design template for you to design a learning space that engages/energizes, focus, and calms your students' brains
- ready-to-use instructional resources for a meaningful and lasting learning experience
- a master class taught by me
- templates for annual, unit, and daily lesson plans
- a simple and fun unit for your students to learn about their brain parts and functions, and *how they learn*!
- and many more resources to help you save time in your efforts to create lasting learning.

https://yanina-s-school.thinkific.com/courses/brainfriendlyteacherbookresources

Social Media

Follow me on social media, where I post short videos and images explaining concepts from this book and weekly tips to use right away in your classroom for meaningful and lasting learning! You can also send me messages and questions through the following platforms! I will be so happy to connect with you!

Instagram: @lets.celebrate.learning

Facebook Group:
https://www.facebook.com/groups/braintipsforyourclassroom

Twitter: @yaninajimenez01

TikTok: @braintipsforteachers

YouTube: Brain-friendly Teacher

LinkedIn: Yanina Jimenez

Bring me as a presenter!!

Send me an email to letscelebratelearning1@gmail.com to inquire about my in-person and online presentations, PD day, and workshops for your conference, district, school, or community.

I can customize my sessions to meet your teachers' and students' needs. All my presentations are research-based and filled with practical strategies to implement right away in your classroom for meaningful, true, and lasting learning.

I can't wait to meet you!

Yanina

https://**BrainFriendlyTeacher**.wordpress.com/

Acknowledgments

To the 5 am hour, thank you for making this book possible. There were sometimes when I was not looking forward to seeing you on my alarm clock. There were other times when I couldn't wait for you to appear on it. So, it has been a wild ride with you. Thank you for showing up each morning to remind me that I have made a promise to finish this book. Sorry for ignoring you some mornings! I am glad you kept showing up each day for me. I would not have done it without you. All the other times during the day were not helpful for me and this book, but you were perfect for my mom, teacher, and student schedules! Thank you again! Until next time. I hope not to see you anytime soon, though. Don't take it personally! I will miss this time in silence with my thoughts, but I rather sleep a little bit longer! I am sure we will cross paths again!

Diego, thank you for your constant support, for always listening to my ideas and responding with, "How can I help you?" For always being concerned about my health, reminding me to slow down while not giving up on my dreams. It has been a wild and beautiful ride with you, almost 30 places lived, and hundreds visited... all because we never forgot the promise to be adventurous in pursuing God's calling for our lives. L.P.Q.T.A.M.X.L.E!

Gloria, I always thank Jesus for bringing you into this world to be part of our family. You are the one who helped your parents settle down in one place, and it has been so worth it!!! I love our conversations, and your many hugs and kisses. I love watching you write prayers in your journal, kneeling by your bed, being so creative, enjoying traveling as much as your parents do, and being such a loving and caring big sister. Your smiles and energy feed me every single day. You are everything to me. Te amo tanto, Lolita!

Andrés, from the moment you entered this world, you got me with your smiles and personality. You have the best sense of humor I have ever seen in a human. You are always happy, inventing something, taking things apart, thinking about numbers, singing beautiful songs to Jesus, and so ready to go on an adventure with your dear Dino! I love your hugs, kisses, and how sweet you are to me. You are everything to me. Te amo tanto, Ané!

Mamá, thank you for showing me how to be humble, a hard worker, and empathetic human. Thank you for modeling how moms can be so close to their children. If I become just a fraction of the kind of mom you are, I made it! Thank you for always praying for me, listening to my stories, problems, projects, everything. Te amo tanto, mami!

Mamá, gracias por mostrarme como ser humilde, trabajadora, empatética, y como las madres pueden ser tan pegadas a sus hijos. Si llego a hacer sólo una fracción de la clase de mamá que sos, la hice! Gracias por siempre orar por mí, escuchar mis historias, problemas, proyectos, todo! Te amo tanto, mami!

Papá, thank you for showing me how to work hard, figure out solutions, and how to be a great dad. You have gone through a lot, yet you keep showing up in life to be an example for your grandchildren and me. I want you in my life forever! Te amo tanto, papi!

Papá, gracias por mostrarme como trabajar duro, buscar soluciones, y como ser un gran papá. Pasaste por mucho, sin embargo, seguís mostrándole la cara a la vida para ser un ejemplo para tus nietos y yo. Espero tenerte muchos años más en mi vida! Te amo tanto, papi!

Acknowledgements

Gustavo, Ivonne, and Nikki: visiting you and receiving your visits have become one of the favorite things in the world to me and now to my children. You are the right definition of family. You are in the good, the bad, the ugly, the great, the ups and the downs of our walk on this planet. I am so blessed to have you close. Los amo tanto, Gusti, Ivi & Nikki!

Mari, Pedro, Tefan, and Gigi: traveling together has been one of my favorite things in this world. I never knew that I needed that so much. Every time I see you, little sister, my heart is complete. Mari, I am constantly learning from your humble and self-giving heart. Te amo tanto, Maruchi!

Dr. Horton, you have heard this so many times from me. Good thing that I will never get tired of reminding you that I am here because of your opportunity when no one knew me. You took a chance, gave me my first job in the United States, and always believed in me. I don't know what you saw in me yet, but I thank God everything single day for that opportunity. My family and I love you so much.

Belén, thank you for all your help and for always going above and beyond. I hope I can meet you someday "para tomar unos mates!"

To all the amazing researchers on Educational Neuroscience, thank you for caring about the education system, our students, and teachers. Thank you for spending countless hours researching the science of teaching and learning!

To all the podcasters and authors who keep sharing their knowledge on the internet for free. Thank you for helping me do this! I couldn't have done it without the massive information and help you put into the world for free! Thank you!

To my students, thank you for showing such passion for learning! YOU are my inspiration. Thank you for always showing up, doing your best, loving learning, helping me improve as a teacher, being great friends, and always showing enthusiasm to learn new things! You are a blessing to me!

To my School, Conference, Union, and Division family: thank you for allowing me to try new and old things in my classroom. Thank you for all the support, love, understanding, enthusiasm, and care you show to my students and me. You make all the difference in my personal and professional life. You are seriously amazing!

Jesus, I would never have done it or been here without you. I am a miracle since my first month on this planet and I continue to be because of you. Thank you for **creating** my brain and my fascination for it! I love you so much.

References

Agarwal, P. K., & Bain, P. M. (2019). Powerful Teaching: Unleash the Science of Learning. San Francisco, CA: Jossey-Bass.

Alford, K. (2019). The rise of infographics: Why teachers and teacher educators should take heed. *Teaching/Writing: The Journal of Writing Teacher Education, 7*(1). https://scholarworks.wmich.edu/wte/vol7/iss1/7

Anand. The Neuroscience: Why Your Brain Loves Good Storytelling https://humanisethebrand.com/neuroscience-storytelling/

Bailey, C. (2017, July 25). *How to calculate your biological prime time - the time of the day you're the most productive.* A Life of Productivity. https://alifeofproductivity.com/calculate-biological-prime-time/

Barker, M. M. (2021). *Brain breaks improve student behavior and focus.* NWCommons. https://nwcommons.nwciowa.edu/education_masters/273/

Briggs, S. (2014). *How to make learning relevant to your students (and why it's crucial to their success).* InformED. https://www.opencolleges.edu.au/informed/features/how-to-make-learning-relevant/

Brown, P. C., Iii, H. R. L., & McDaniel, M. A. (2014b). *Make It Stick: The Science of Successful Learning* (1st ed.). Belknap Press: An Imprint of Harvard University Press.

Bruer, J. (1997). Education and the brain: A bridge too far. *Educational Researcher, 26*(8), 4–16. https://www.jsmf.org/about/j/education_and_brain.pdf

Caine, Caine, G., McClintic, C., & Klimek, K. J. (2009). *12 brain/mind learning principles in action.* SAGE Publications.

Cappello, K. (2020, December 21). *The impact of sleep on learning and memory | chronobiology and sleep institute | Perelman school of medicine at the university of Pennsylvania.* Perelman School of Medicine - University of Pennsylvania. https://www.med.upenn.edu/csi/the-impact-of-sleep-on-learning-and-memory.html

Carson, R. (2017). *The sense of wonder: A celebration of nature for parents and children.* Harper Perennial.

Cherry, Kendra (2020) What Is the Hippocampus? Medically reviewed by Shaheen Lakhan, MD, Ph.D., FAAN. https://www.verywellmind.com/what-is-the-hippocampus

Chiaro, C. (2021, September 29). *How to utilize hexagonal thinking with your students.* TeachHUB. https://www.teachhub.com/teaching-strategies/2021/05/how-to-utilize-hexagonal-thinking-with-your-students/

Clark, M. (2021, August 4). *What is dual coding theory and how can it help teaching?* CENTURY. https://www.century.tech/news/what-is-dual-coding-theory-and-how-can-it-help-teaching/

Clear, J. (2018). *Atomic habits: tiny changes, remarkable results: an easy & proven way to build good habits & break bad ones.* New York, New York: Avery, an imprint of Penguin Random House.

Cooper, B. B. (2013, May 16). *Why getting new things makes us feel so good: Novelty and the brain.* Buffer Resources. https://buffer.com/resources/novelty-and-the-brain-how-to-learn-more-and-improve-your-memory/

Dabbs, A. (2019, March 22). *Indoor plants for the classroom.* Home & Garden Information Center | Clemson University, South Carolina. https://hgic.clemson.edu/indoor-plants-for-the-classroom/

Dave. (2020, July 14). *The scientifically-proven benefits of daydreaming.* Naked Reverie. https://nakedreverie.com/the-scientifically-proven-benefits-of-daydreaming/

Doran, G. (1981, November). *SMART Goals.* Management Review.

Ellenbogen, J. M., Payne, J. D., & Stickgold, R. (2006). *Sleep, learning, and memory.* Healthy Sleep Med Harvard.

https://healthysleep.med.harvard.edu/healthy/matters/benefits-of-sleep/learning-memory

Ferguson, J., & Ferguson, D. (2019, November 12). *The five steps of leadership development*. Transforming Leader. https://transformingleader.org/five-steps-of-leadership-development/

Fisher, A. V., Godwin, K. E., & Seltman, H. (2014). *Visual Environment, Attention Allocation, and Learning in Young Children*. Psychological Science, 25(7), 1362–1370. https://doi.org/10.1177/0956797614533801

Ford, D. J. (2011, July 20). *How the brain learns*. Training Industry. https://trainingindustry.com/articles/content-development/how-the-brain-learns/

Gaab. (2016). *Reading and the brain*. Harvard Medical School. https://hms.harvard.edu/news-events/publications-archive/brain/reading-brain

Gallo, C. (2015). *Talk Like TED: The 9 Public-Speaking Secrets of the World's Top Minds* (Reprint ed.). St. Martin's Griffin.

gigasavvy.com/how-to-use-the-rule-of-three-to-create-better-marketing-content/

Great Schools Partnership. (2016, February 18). *Student engagement definition*. The Glossary of Education Reform. https://www.edglossary.org/student-engagement/

Grotzer, T. (n.d.). *Giving students enough space and time to reflect*. Instructional Moves. https://instructionalmoves.gse.harvard.edu/giving-students-enough-space-and-time-reflect

Guy-Evans, O. (2021a, April 15). *Prefrontal lobe: Definition, functions, and location*. Simply Psychology. https://www.simplypsychology.org/prefontal-lobe.html

H, Meg. (2018). *Art increases empathy, tolerance, and feelings of love*. Toluna Influencers - Opinions for All. https://za.toluna.com/opinions/3950695/Art-increases-empathy,-

tolerance,-and-feelings-of-love

Hammond, Z. L. (2015). *Culturally responsive teaching and the brain.* Corwin Press.

Heavily decorated classrooms disrupt attention and learning in young children. (2014, May 27). Association for Psychological Science - APS. https://www.psychologicalscience.org/news/releases/heavily-decorated-classrooms-disrupt-attention-and-learning-in-young-children.html

Heller, S. (2015, July 9). *The cognitive benefits of doodling.* The Atlantic. https://www.theatlantic.com/entertainment/archive/2015/07/doodling-for-cognitive-benefits/398027/

Hill, N. (1939). *Think and grow rich.* The Ralston Society, Meriden, Conn.

Howard-Jones (2010). *Introducing Neuroeducational Research.* Routledge.

Huizen, J. (2021, October 29). *What to know about short-term and long-term memory loss.* https://www.Medicalnewstoday.Com/. Retrieved June 2022, from https://www.medicalnewstoday.com/articles/memory-loss

The importance of whitespace in education. (2019, August 22). ResourcED - A Promethean Blog. https://resourced.prometheanworld.com/whitespace-education/

Jacobi-Vessels Jill, L. (2013). Discovering nature: The benefits of teaching outside of the classroom. *Dimensions of Early Childhood, 41*(3), 4–10. https://eric.ed.gov/?id=EJ1044065

Jensen, E. (2005). *Teaching with the brain in mind* (ed.). ASCD.

Jensen, E. (2019, December 7). *Getting everyone on the same page: How YOUR classroom can experience "Brain synchronicity."* Jensen Learning. https://www.jensenlearning.com/getting-everyone-on-the-same-page-how-your-classroom-can-experience-brain-synchronicity/

Jensen, E., & McConchie, L. (2020). *Brain-Based learning: Teaching the way students really learn.* Amsterdam University Press.

Jones, A. (2019, December 17). *How we can bring creativity and imagination back to the classroom.* PBS Education.

https://www.pbs.org/education/blog/how-we-can-bring-creativity-and-imagination-back-to-the-classroom

Jones, H. P. (2009). *Introducing neuroeducational research: Neuroscience, education and the brain from contexts to practice* (1st ed.). Routledge.

Joseph, N. (2003). Metacognition in the Classroom: Examining Theory and Practice. *Pedagogy Duke University Press, 3*(1), 109–113. https://doi.org/10.1215/15314200-3-1-109

Keep your brain young with music. (2021). Johns Hopkins Medicine. https://www.hopkinsmedicine.org/health/wellness-and-prevention/keep-your-brain-young-with-music

Kiser, S. (2020, December 17). *The benefits of student choice.* TeachHUB. https://www.teachhub.com/professional-development/2020/12/the-benefits-of-student-choice/

Koch, W. (2013, January 7). *15 reasons why daydreamers are better learners.* InformED. https://www.opencolleges.edu.au/informed/features/15-reasons-why-daydreamers-are-better-learners/

Landhuis, E. (2015, September 30). *Stuffy classrooms may lower test scores.* Science News for Students. https://www.sciencenewsforstudents.org/article/stuffy-classrooms-may-lower-test-scores

Ledbury, R., White, I., & Darn, S. (2004). The importance of eye contact in the classroom. *The Internet TESL Journal, X*(8).

Lynch, M. (2019, September 5). *How to train students to use their prefrontal cortex to pay better attention.* The Edvocate. https://www.theedadvocate.org/how-to-train-students-to-use-their-prefrontal-cortex-to-pay-better-attention/

Maich, K., Davies, A. W. J., & van Rhijn, T. (2018). A relaxation station in every location. *Intervention in School and Clinic, 54*(3), 160–165. https://doi.org/10.1177/1053451218767916

Mazarin, J. (2021, September 27). *Attention as part of cognitive development: Definition & process* [Video]. Study.Com. https://study.com/academy/lesson/attention-as-part-of-cognitive-development-definition-process.html

McDonald Connor, C., Graham, S., Kang, S., & Mancilla-Martinez, J. (2020). *Literacy 4–6: Long-term memory*. Digital Promise. https://lvp.digitalpromiseglobal.org/content-area/literacy-4-6/factors

Memory consolidation. (2020). The Human Memory. https://human-memory.net/memory-consolidation/#Basics_of_Memory_Consolidation

Minahan, J. (2019, October 1). *Trauma-Informed teaching strategies*. ASCD. https://www.ascd.org/el/articles/trauma-informed-teaching-strategies

Moss, M., Hewitt, S., Moss, L., & Wesnes, K. (2008). Modulation of cognitive performance and mood by aromas of peppermint and ylang-ylang. *International Journal of Neuroscience, 118*(1), 59–77. https://doi.org/10.1080/00207450601042094

Neely, C. (2019, August 23). *Using Open-Ended questions in the classroom*. Teach Stone. http://info.teachstone.com/blog/open-ended-questions-in-the-classroom

Nelson-Danley, K. (2021, May 26). *How to Utilize Hexagonal Thinking with Your Students*. https://www.Teachhub.Com/. Retrieved June 2022, from https://www.teachhub.com/teaching-strategies/2021/05/how-to-utilize-hexagonal-thinking-with-your-students/

Newport, C. (2016). *Deep work: Rules for focused success in a distracted world*. Grand Central Publishing.

Oakley, B., & Schewe, O. (2021). *Learn like a pro: Science-Based tools to become better at anything*. St. Martin's Essentials.

Opitz, M. F., & Ford, M. P. (2014). *Engaging Minds in the Classroom: The Surprising Power of Joy*. ASCD.

Osgood-Campbell, E. (2015, March 1). *Investigating the educational implications of embodied cognition: A model interdisciplinary inquiry in mind, brain, and education curricula*. Wiley Online Library. https://onlinelibrary.wiley.com/doi/abs/10.1111/mbe.12063

Ostroff, W. L. (2016). *Cultivating Curiosity in K-12 Classrooms: How to*

Promote and Sustain Deep Learning. ASCD.

Parker, F., Novak, J., & Bartell, T. (2017, October 1). *To engage students, give them meaningful choices in the classroom*. Phi Delta Kappan - The Professional Journal for Educators. https://kappanonline.org/engage-students-give-meaningful-choices-classroom/

Phillips, K. (2017, November 4). *How to use silence as a teaching tool*. The Art of Education University. https://theartofeducation.edu/2017/11/06/silence-teaching-tool/

Posey, A. (2018). *Engage the Brain: How to Design for Learning That Taps into the Power of Emotion*. ASCD.

Ramirez, A. (2015, April 29). *5 reasons why origami improves students' skills*. Edutopia. https://www.edutopia.org/blog/why-origami-improves-students-skills-ainissa-ramirez

Roberson, R. (2013, September). *Helping students find relevance*. APA.Org. https://www.apa.org/ed/precollege/ptn/2013/09/students-relevance

Schomaker, J., & Meeter, M. (2015). Short- and long-lasting consequences of novelty, deviance and surprise on brain and cognition. *Neuroscience & Biobehavioral Reviews, 55,* 268–279. https://doi.org/10.1016/j.neubiorev.2015.05.002.

Schweighofer, J. (2022). The Benefits of Journaling in the Classroom. Https://Upub.Net/. Retrieved June 2022, from https://upub.net/blog/the-benefits-of-journaling/

Sjøgren, K. (2021, July 13). *How the brain consolidates information while you rest*. Science News. https://sciencenews.dk/en/how-the-brain-consolidates-information-while-you-rest

Sousa, D. A. (2011). *Educational neuroscience*. Corwin Publishers.

Sousa, D. A. (2011). *How the brain learns* (Fourth ed.). Corwin.

Sousa, D. A. (2016). *Engaging the rewired brain*. Learning Sciences International.

Stenger, M. (2014, August 6). *5 Research-Based tips for providing* students with meaningful feedback. Edutopia. https://www.edutopia.org/blog/tips-providing-students-meaningful-feedback-marianne-stenger

Sumeracki, M. (2020, February 22). *Elaboration as self-explanation.* The Learning Scientists. https://www.learningscientists.org/blog/2020/2/20-1

Suzuki, W. (2018, February 28). *The brain-changing benefits of exercise* [Video]. TED Talks. https://www.ted.com/talks/wendy_suzuki_the_brain_changing_benefits_of_exercise?language=en

Terada, Y. (2017, September 20). *Why Students Forget—and What You Can Do About It.* https://www.Edutopia.Org/. https://www.edutopia.org/article/why-students-forget-and-what-you-can-do-about-it

Universal Plublishing, & Schweighofer, J. (2019, July 3). *The benefits of journaling in the classroom.* Universal Publishing Blog. https://upub.net/blog/the-benefits-of-journaling/

van Braam, H. (2021). *The psychology of colors and their meanings.* Color Psychology. https://www.colorpsychology.org/

Watson, A. C. (2021). *The Goldilocks Map: A classroom teacher's quest to evaluate 'brain-based' teaching advice.* John Catt Educational.

Weinstein, Y., Sumeracki, M., & Caviglioli, O. (2019). *Understanding How We Learn: A Visual Guide* (1st ed.). Routledge.

Wells, G., & Arauz, R. M. (2006a). Dialogue in the classroom. *Journal of the Learning Sciences, 15*(3), 379–428. https://doi.org/10.1207/s15327809jls1503_3

Wheeler, S. (2022). *The flow theory in the classroom: A primer.* TeachThought. https://www.teachthought.com/learning/flow-theory-classroom-primer/

Williams, M. (2020, November 12). *6 types of learning goals for students.* Classcraft Blog. https://www.classcraft.com/blog/learning-goals-for-students/

Winerman, L. (2005). The mind's mirror: A new type of neuron--called a mirror neuron--could help explain how we learn through mimicry and why we empathize with others. *Monitor Staff, 36*(9), 48. https://www.apa.org/monitor/oct05/mirror

Yale - Poorvu Center for Teaching and learning. (n.d.). *Reflective teaching*. The Poorvu Center. https://poorvucenter.yale.edu/ReflectiveTeaching

Zack, P. J. (2014, October 28). *Why your brain loves good storytelling*. Harvard Business Review. https://hbr.org/2014/10/why-your-brain-loves-good-storytelling

Zadina, J. N. (2015). The emerging role of educational neuroscience in education reform. *Psicología Educativa, 21*(2), 71–77. https://doi.org/10.1016/j.pse.2015.08.005

Made in the USA
Monee, IL
12 October 2022